Herbivores AND CARNIVORES

The Struggle for Democratic
Cultural Values in post-War Britain

Essays and Papers

John Astley

Information Årchitects
2008

First Published in the United Kingdom in 2008
by INFORMATION ARCHITECTS
an imprint of IA Ltd
www.iAimprint.com

© John Astley 2008

John Astley has asserted his right under the Copyright,
Designs and Patents Act 1988.

ISBN- (10): 0-9551834-3-X
ISBN- (13): 978-0-9551834-3-0

British Library Cataloguing in Publication Data.
A catalogue record for this book is available from the British Library.

Classification: Non-Fiction
Social Sciences/Cultural Studies/
Britain (since 1945)

BIC Codes
J/JB

Bibliographic Data also available:
Nielsen Book Data

Typeset in Palatino Linotype

Front/back cover image: © Andrezej Krauze
Title page image: from *The Elephant's Child* (or How the
Elephant got its trunk) by Rudyard Kipling in the *Just So Stories*
(1902)

Herbivores and Carnivores
The Struggle for Democratic Cultural Values in post-War Britain

John Astley

In *Herbivores and Carnivores,* John Astley offers his insights for a closed or cloaked subject: the struggle for democratic cultural values in modern Britain.

A central theme emerges: as individual members of society, we so often seem to adhere - the author suggests - to strictly limited choices with pre-packaged versions of the way we live our lives.

If this is so, then why, and from where, do cultural values spring? Whose interests are being promoted? Who writes the scripts?

In his flagship essay, the author explores this complex issue, which seems to have slipped from view in today's media-drenched consumer society. If cultural values - *i.e.*, what is, and what is not, important - have become eroded or obviated by consumerism, then is it not time to ask again: whose interests are being promoted? And why?

For that matter, who are the Herbivores and Carnivores of the ongoing struggle as cited in the author's beguiling title?

The reader is offered a cud or two to chew on, while ruminating over the larger fodder of the themes presented in these essays and papers.

*

John Astley is a sociologist, lecturer, and writer - and a frequent contributor to journals, conferences, and radio talks. As a sociologist of culture, he is the author of three volumes of collected essays: *Liberation and Domestication, Culture and Creativity*, and *Professionalism and Practice* - as well as a noted monograph on The Beatles phenomenon from a cultural studies perspective.

By the same author:

Liberation and Domestication (Essays 1)
Culture and Creativity (Essays 2)
Professionalism and Practice (Essays 3)

Why Don't We Don't We Do It In The Road?
The Beatles Phenomenon Explained

Contents

This book is dedicated to all those educators in the struggle for democratic cultural values; and, in the words of *AB*, have done their best to 'pass it on'.

Front/back cover image: courtesy Andrezej Krauze, whose inspirational work can regularly be found in *The Guardian* newspaper.

BIBLIOGRAPHIC NOTES:

The original version of 'Herbivores versus Carnivores' was presented as a talk for 'Cultural Returns: assessing the place of culture in social thought', organised by the Open University's Pavis Centre for Research and held in Oxford on 19 September 2002. The paper later appeared in the author's *Culture and Creatvity* (2006) as did 'Raymond Williams: a biographical profile' (*c*. 1989). The essay 'Youth Service Policy Making in the 1950s' (*c*. 1987), which is reproduced here with permission of the National Youth Agency, appeared in the author's *Liberation and Domestication* (2006), as did 'Being an Agent of Change' (c. 1992). The essay 'Professions, Professionals, and Power' is an excerpt from 'The New Professionals' (c. 1989), which was published in the author's *Professionalism and Practice* (2006).

Preface

How, then, did Herbivores and Carnivores originate? A kind of biological process - or evolution, anyway - is involved. In the autumn of 2002, I wrote a paper by that title for an Open University conference in Oxford, which I thought might satisfy my curiosity on the subject of the struggle for cultural dominance implicit in the title of the piece; but, instead, my own curiosity drove me on.

The focal point for the post-mortem investigation is located in a space somewhere between my value orientation and my vocabulary of motives.

What is my motive?

As a starting place, I have reconsidered the issues that were raised in that conference talk, along with a reassessment of my motivation for writing that paper in the first place.

The struggle for democratic values in contemporary life, the means of getting there, and what stands in the way, is never far from my consciousness, and so I determined to return to these concerns. What I wrote, and said, in 2002, and what I have written now, is very much 'work in progress', and this collection of pieces inevitably poses more question than it answers.

The present narrative is then an attempt - still evolving - to investigate the nature of democratic cultural values. Whose influence is greater on the way we live our lives? The Herbivores or the Carnivores?

As I write this, there is a good deal of discussion as to whether democracy is in decline in Britain, and if indeed there is a democratic deficit in our lives. Moreover, what is actually being mourned is not democracy, because we have never had it, but the loss of that hope we had in achieving a democratic life.

J.A.
Devon, 2008

Herbivores versus Carnivores
The struggle for democratic cultural
values in Britain after 1945

In the winter of 1978-9, I sat down to write a long essay on
'The Beatles Phenomenon'.[1] I sought in that piece to pose,
and answer to my own satisfaction, a series of questions
about the nature of popular cultures in post-War Britain,
which the rise of The Beatles epitomised.

My main question was why, and how, could a cultural
phenomenon like The Beatles happen? My approach was a
socio-historical one, identifying significant transformation
for example, and linked to my role as a critical theorist, and
a devotee of Raymond Williams. Despite the many failings
of that work, I would still stand by a good deal of what was
said; and, essentially for my writing thereafter, this is how I
came to explore the broader issues of cultural values. In
discussing the cultural antecedents of that pop phenomenon
I opened up, and developed in a definite political context,
questions about the increasing domination, indeed colo-
nisation, of popular cultures by the commercial nexus. These
processes, aided and abetted by those with political power
(in whose interest it was and remains), help to create and
preside over a largely emasculated and stultified population.

One of the issues I addressed then was the way a
revitalised consumerist and liberal-looking capitalism could
present a feeling of openness while actually maintaining the
traditional privileges of the elites. 'Post-War settlement'?

---

[1] *Why Don't We Do It In the Road* (2006)

Yes. Greater democracy? An emphatic: No. I am reminded of those earnest debates in the 1960s about class, parenting, and schooling, seeking to find some State-sponsored and acceptable solution to the continued failings of a class-ridden and despotic schooling system. Consider how the 'common-sense' message of Plowden in 1967 about the deprivation, disadvantage, and cultural deficit experienced by working class children required a compensatory educational facelift. As Basil Bernstein pointed out in his 1971 essay 'Education Cannot Compensate for Society', the audacity of the already privileged to blame the working class for their failings was quite staggering. Please note that the educational policy arm of the New Labour State apparatus is referring to social class as a key factor in life chances once again. Is this an appropriate time to re-publish Michael Young's *The Rise of the Meritocracy* (1958)?

The title of this paper comes from the essay 'Festival' by Michael Frayn, the final piece in *Age of Austerity 1945-51* edited by Michael Sissons and Philip French in 1963. (The year of publication just happens to coincide with the breakthrough into international celebrity of The Beatles). Frayn's essay is about the intense political and cultural-values struggle to create The Festival of Britain held in 1951 (to which I went as a seven-year old). Frayn used the terms 'herbivores and carnivores' to identify the two sides battling it out for the very existence of the Festival. He characterises the Herbivores as philanthropic, kindly, whimsical, cosy, optimistic, and middlebrow. The Carnivores were 'the other side of the coin'; and, as Frayn says of them, 'If God had not wished them (the main body of the upper and middle classes) to prey on all smaller and weaker creatures without scruple he would not have made them as they are'.

I certainly would not want to subscribe to all of the Herbivore characteristics, because they did in the main see the working class as the inert objects of benign administration. However, I am certainly prepared to start here as part of a debate about what, and whose, values do matter - and why. Many of our contemporary 'the Great and the Good' along with the 'woolly liberals' much derided by Stalinists like Jack Straw, qualify as Herbivores. It is certainly the case that New Labour has come to power on the back of the forty-year triumph of the Carnivores. New Labour politics is the most recent phase of taking democratic dialogue further and further away from the ordinary people, and the Herbivores alike.

One of my aims here is to argue for a debate, yes, dialogue, certainly, about cultural values, and the lack of opportunity that most of us have to engage with ideas, our own, and those of others. Habermas' communicative action thesis (1984) is an issue here. Our lives are dominated by an advanced consumer-oriented global capitalism, which as an entity relies on our choices being manipulated and circumscribed in the interests of big profits and continued economic and cultural domination. (Much as described by Marx in volume three of *Capital*, published by Engels in 1894). This domination is supplemented by a system of quasi-representative government that is oppressive because it deals in propaganda, the processes of which are oligarchic and opaque rather than open and transparent - as is always claimed in the propaganda. The recent television series *The*

Century of the Self (BBC2, 2002) written by Andrew Curtis brought these and other issues out very well, and should remind us of the pioneering work of Vance Packard, who, in *The Hidden Persuaders* (1957), for example, drew our attention to 'the packaged soul'.

I want to argue that we are (still) alienated because of the separation from the fruits of our labour or any genuine sense of working for an inter-related personal and social fulfilment. We work for wages, to be choice-making consumers, to be permitted to engage with unbounded joy in the status-acquisition rush by spending money we do not have. I see no reason to alter much the 'one dimensional man' thesis of Herbert Marcuse (1964), namely that 'the technology of advanced industrial societies has enabled them to eliminate conflict by assimilating all those who in earlier forms of social order provided either voices or forces of dissent. Technology does this partly by creating affluence. Freedom from material want, which Marx and Marcuse himself took and take to be the precondition of other freedoms, has been transformed into an agency for producing servitude.' (MacIntyre, 1970). Now although this 1964 thesis was pessimistic, and overtaken by many subsequent political upheavals apparently demonstrating people's capacity to throw off their psychological as well as political chains (the collapse of Stalinism being a case in point), I would argue that the servitude remains. Neil Postman, the American Sociologist, suggested that we are 'amusing ourselves to death' (1986); and, in his essay, 'A Sad Heart at the Supermarket', Randall Jarrell argued that half of us is stuffed to death, while the other half is starved to death

(1962). Both self and society!

I want to argue that far from escaping the servitude that comes with the 'freedoms' that advanced capitalism provides, we are more and more in debt to these power sources and forces. Look, for instance, at the withering authority of the 'lifestyle' role modelling which is now part of the daily routine of the mass media.

In the wake of my essay on The Beatles, I went on to write about the increasing power of what I called Ideological Cultural Apparatuses (ICAs), the everyday mechanisms by which our commonplace and regularly used ideas, images, and values are recycled for our endless 'entertainment', or titillation. Here we are flattered, have our strings pulled, and generally praise ourselves for being so clever; hedonism and solipsism combined in self-actualisation! We are, of course, constantly on the cusp of consuming some new, and essential, thing; another example in this age of information of more knowledge without wisdom.

However, despite all this, I do remain optimistic, and my interest in these cultural processes has been stimulated over many years by the likes of Zygmunt Bauman, who has encouraged me to write and talk about cultural creativity as an antidote to alienation (1976). This also takes me close to the grounded aesthetics and common culture ideas of Paul Willis, also creating a thought on our conference title as apposite. Culture has two senses here, as a functioning analytical concept in understanding social thought, and also as the social reality of cultural actions in everyday life, much in the 'common culture' vein.

There are many social and cultural institutions that can e

seen as ICAs, among them the BBC and other agencies of mass media communication. There are the universities. There are the culture-heritage industries that grow by the day, which have the gall to take what passes for people's real lives (and usually oppressed ones at that), and transform them before our eyes into packages of homogenised history bites, which offer up a simulated version of life in an easily digestible format. Even here in the forms of contemporary domestication 'we' cannot be allowed to work our minds too hard. It is also worth reminding ourselves that 'history' is written for consumption today. So, we need to ask: which values are being promoted, and why?

What is at stake here - when there are those who have the power to set agendas? We are not simply talking about the power individuals and organisations have to command obedience, but the way they consistently create the contexts around access and opportunity, about democratic decision-making, or the lack of it. Discourses are shaped; even the idea of having a dialogue around alternatives is marginalized.

For several years at Open University summer school, I had the pleasure of giving a regularly updated talk on 'Six Propositions about Culture and Identity'. These six were:

1. It is to be welcomed that the UK is a more multi-cultural society (when there are continuity as well as change issues).
2. Human action creates culture, contributing to the personal and social expressions of identity.

3. Culture reflects the diversity and semi-autonomy of 'us'. . .

4. But, there are contradictions and conflicts which arise. People's aspirations *versus* forces of control.; struggles occur, often located in particular sites.

5. However, people invariably feel that their needs can only be met by engaging in these struggles

6. Culture as articulated opposition to exclusion, and these marginal cultures as an antidote to alienation and oppression.

These talks always provoked intense, interested, debates. The dialogue rumbled on afterward for some time, and I always felt that they unleashed a genuine desire among a very diverse group of people to argue and speculate about contemporary society and utopian visions. The very openness of such culturally heterogeneous groups of people brought together in a wonderful educational spirit always seemed to me to be resources of hope.

We have in this country a robust and innovative tradition of studying culture in all respects. This is a radical intellectual tradition, built on the foundations of a radical oppositional political culture that should not be surrendered just because we are constantly swimming against the tide of philistinism and open hostility from those in power.

II

So, that was the original paper; this is the springboard, and what now follows is a development of the issues that are raised above, which are, in their way, contexts for what was originally written. This may seem like a back-to-front way of setting out my ideas, but I see it more as an attempt to 'flesh out' the original talk, which in the nature of conference papers needed to be reasonably brief. One of my aims in the original paper was to focus on the public, collective, and 'democratic' aims and nature of certain post-1945 organisations and projects. There are potentially many of these that could serve as examples, to emphasise my point that so much of British life is best done *as* collective, inclusive, in the public domain, and seeking to be democratic enterprises. Some have succeeded, and thrived; others have struggled and failed to achieve their original aspirations. But at least people had the courage, and the critical and utopian vision to try.

One of my key concerns over many years has been the way in which ordinary working people have been seduced by the acquisitive life, a desire to jump on to the hamster wheel of consumer culture. People have been persuaded; often by the leaders of the Labour movement; to see their aspirations in life wedded to their capacity to enter the marketplace and sell their labour at the most advantageous price, and while in that marketplace to consume on the basis of their status-oriented wants. I have raised this issue here and there in these articles because it is such a fundamental question. The politics of selfishness has been able to thrive because so many otherwise decent and reasonable people have had their understandable aspirations for a good quality of life for themselves, and for others, hijacked. People were, and in many cases still are, essentially altruistic in their values, but they have been duped in to diverting their aspirations into the accumulation of things that can bring only temporary solace at best.

In his Introduction to *Building a Better Future* (2000), Robert Elwall offers an optimistic account of modernism and the 1950s: '. . .much had been achieved since 1945 when Labour's electoral victory marked a national determination to create a post-War social order which would be human, equitable, planned and, above all, new: the Welfare State allied to a modernist architecture would help to ensure there would be no return to the grim, depression days of the 1930s.' (Elwall, p.9).

Elwall makes reference to the New Towns Act (1946), and the Town and Country Planning Act (1945), and to the legislation on house building produced by Bevan in his dual capacity as minister for health and housing. He counters this optimism by reminding the reader of the chronic shortage of materials, and the general impression that the period up to the 1951 Festival of Britain was in architectural-style terms the ending of an era rather than the beginning of one. However, Elwall reinforces the view held by many observers of the zeitgeist that: 'To the public, however, it was a revelation. Light, airy, informal and scaled to people, the Festival site seemed less a remembrance of things past, more an intimation of a brighter, modernist future to come.' (Elwall, p.11).

A key issue raised by Elwall was the emphatic shift from a private focus on design practice and building to a public one. The Labour Government's understandable focus on reconstruction saw them limit the private sphere 'by a system of building licences which channelled scarce materials and resources into the priority areas of housing and schools.' (Elwall, p.12). Not surprisingly, therefore, this was an era dominated by local authorities, with by the mid-1950s nearly 50 per cent of architects employed in the public domain. While some architects resented, and resisted this, often arguing that being employed by 'the State' ran contrary to the best traditions of independent professional practice, many others embraced a set of values that took them into this collective practice. There are echoes here of the medical profession, of course, with the BMA arguing in the NHS bill debates that being employed by the State would undermine the traditional relationship between physician and patient!

There is a wealth of engrossing subject material here to explore, all emphasising the cut and thrust of architectural practice, agreed welfare needs, raised expectations about equality of opportunity and access to a more democratically sensitive response to the sharing-out of scarce resources.

The building of Jerusalem in this green and pleasant land, maybe. One area that was most notable in this regard was the school building programme of the post- War years, and I would direct the interested reader to Andrew Saint's book *Towards a Social Architecture: The Role of School Building in Post-War England* (1987)

The next part this essay, if I may pre-empt it so late in

this part, opens with reference to my secondary schooling, and the experience of crossing social class barriers, which was a characteristic rite of passage for many of us born during, and immediately after, the 1939-45 War. As I suggest below, this was an experience reflected across many genres of writing, and especially interestingly so in fiction and drama. The writing of David Storey, say, or Dennis Potter, draws on these 'crossing a river of fire' type of issues. There is also the seminal writing of Raymond Williams, who not only wrote acclaimed critical cultural theory, but also developed his ideas on 'culture and society' *via* his largely autobiographical fiction beginning with *Border Country* in 1960. In the preface, he says: 'I know this country, but the characters and events of the novel are imagined, and are not intended to describe actual persons and events.' How true this is for many of us, where it is even possible that writing in one way or another about the contexts to our past lives, and future hopes, is an attempt at atonement for past mistakes, missed opportunities, lapses of courage, and so on.

III

In the mid-1950s I 'passed' the 11+ Exam, and attended a boys' grammar school - all elbow patches and Gilbert and Sullivan. It was located in a leafy, middle-class suburb on the other side of the south-coast city in which I lived. A double bus-ride only served to confirm the separateness from the lower middle-respectable working class neigh-bourhood that was home. I say 'attended', but in all honesty

I never ever felt completely at ease in that school. I went there and did all the usual school-ish things, and got involved in school-team sport and the like. But? Even at sixteen, I suppose I was reflective enough to acknowledge that the schoolmasters still seemed to be in a state of shock as a consequence of having to take in boys like me.

My experience, and that of my mother, was not all that different from the one described by Jackson and Marsden in their 1962 classic study *Education and the Working Class*. Okay, so their setting was Huddersfield, but the issues were largely the same. I started at this school only eleven years after the 1944 (Butler) Education Act; which had extended free secondary schooling to all children and opened the way for 20 per cent of children to gain a place at a grammar school on the basis of a diagnostic intelligence test. At the time, there were three types of secondary school (grammar, technical, and modern) of this brave new Welfare State era that were allegedly 'equal but different'. However, we should also recall that before the onset of war in 1939, the Labour Party had discussed, and advocated a policy-shift to multilateral (*i.e.*, comprehensive) secondary education, as part of reforms that would provide free secondary education for all children up to sixteen. Labour leadership equivocations with this Party policy soon manifested, for example, the 1943 White Paper on Educational Reconstruction. This policy document accepted the recommendations for a tripartite system, followed within days of the discovery by the Norwood Committee that in fact children were indeed readily recognisable as being in these *three categories*.

The 1945 caretaker Conservative government hastily produced a policy statement 'The Nation's Schools' which accepted a tripartite model, and rejection of multilateralism. After Labour's election in 1945 with a massive majority, with clear policy guidance from the Party Conference, and advice from its specialist advisers like the Advisory Committee on Education (ACE), the new government actually kept close to the Tory policy paper, and rejected multilateral secondary education. It is also worth reminding ourselves that of the 80 per cent turnout for the 1945 election 39 per cent voted for the Tories. So, the Labour party received 47.8 per cent of the vote, but this is yet another reminder of the traditional conservative values of the time, and since (Marwick, 1991).

It is also worth noting that Brian Jackson went on to publish *Streaming: An Education System in Miniature* in 1964. This book is a damning indictment of the whole selection, streaming, banding, setting, and so on, approach to 'sheep and goats' schooling, and should be compulsory reading for the current crop of policy makers. It might help redress their apparent amnesia? I remember very clearly spending most of my primary school days from September to the March preparing for the 11+ Exam, which was taken over two days, but whose effects lasted for years.

In recent years, when discussing differential education achievement, sociologists have made much of the concept of 'cultural capital'. In brief, this idea suggests that children inherit know-how, insights, expectations, and goal-career related aspirations and orientations, from their parents. These assets are to be re-invested in the future; speculation it may be, but all within a closely observed set of means and ends that has relevance for the participants. One of the reasons why middle class children in post-War Britain have done so well in education, and been able, just about, to maintain their inherited privileges, is mainly because of 'cultural capital'.

At the end of my first term at grammar school, my father died. He was a very intelligent and well-educated man, and had been very excited at the prospect of my grammar school career. He would have been a great source of support, guidance, and an appropriate mixture of socialization and social control, keeping me informed and focused. My mother was a wonderful person who gave me an enormous amount of emotional support as well as continuing to meet my other everyday welfare needs. However, her background was rural working class, and when it came to coping with a son at a grammar school she didn't have a clue.

I am certain that my experience, then and since, has been echoed in the lives of many thousands of young people, and serves to emphasise just how crucial is our individual and collective experience of schooling. One of the key issues here is the inter-relationship between the social structure of schooling for each child and young person, and the agency, or choice(s) that that person actually possesses. A fundamental aspect of the maturing process is for us to be able to work on, and work out, who we are, who do we want to become, and which social institutions, social relationships, and so on, are to play a part in the shaping of our identity. The inter-relationship between our identity, sense of self; who *we* think we are, and our social identity, who *other people* think we are, is crucial for our life - and life chances.

The role of (critical) theory is of obvious importance here because it seeks to go beyond formal political analysis to understand how politics inserts itself into the life of individual subjects. And, as I shall keep arguing, we all take actions, but not necessarily in conditions of our choosing. The inter-relation between social structure, our character, and our agency, is a fertile domain for consideration. In my original 'Herbivores versus Carnivores' piece, I made a passing reference to the 1960-70s arguments on 'cultural deprivation', and those earnest debates about class, parenting, and schooling, and the under-achievement of so many children. In the Plowden Report (1967), much was said about the disadvantages faced by many working class children as a consequence of their class-culture background. It was argued that for many children there was a 'seamless web of circumstances' related to their working class culture, language, parenting, and neighbourhood, that reinforced norms, and expectations, the cumulative local experience of limited schooling, and so on. In short, this was a know-your-place ethos deeply established in the 'gene pool' that prevented children from day one of their schooling experience from 'tuning in to' this new, and usually alien, cultural *milieu*. The Labour government of Harold Wilson 'inherited' Plowden, and it was another pinprick in the assumed cosiness of life in the 'soar-away Sixties', a further big question mark placed against the conventional wisdom of 'the open society'. Like many, or even most, aspects of welfare state provision, the twenty years of the reality of massive inequalities were still recurring by the day. Educational Priority Areas (EPAs) were established in areas of the greatest identified need (inner city areas in the main), and extra resources were diverted to schooling as a solution (see Eric Midwinter's *Priority Education*, 1972). Social democratic academics were much in favour of these developments, these policy and practice responses, to the joint failure of a market-linked welfarism and entrenched working class fatalism, even obduracy. A. H. Halsey, the Oxford University academic, was typical of those researchers who genuinely believed that these forms of targeted interventions could solve the problem. Other researchers disagreed, notably Basil Bernstein, who wrote from a Durkheimian perspective that schools were 'cultural repeaters'. The very point of the schooling system, both public and private, was to reproduce traditional and dominant values in Britain. All children were expected to conform to these aims whether it made sense to them or not. Schools were not required to make much, if any adjustments, and 1940s-type thinking on fixed aptitudes and attitudes were exposed once again. 'In no field has the division of the British people into social classes been more clearly demonstrated than in education. Throughout history the middle and upper classes, through their control of the economic, legislative and administrative apparatus, have given to the working classes as little and as poor an education as possible.' (*Education for Democracy*, Rubinstein & Stoneman, Eds., 1970). Bernstein argued in his 1971 *New Society* article that 'education cannot compensate for society', and, ten years or so later, even the likes of Halsey had to agree that this was probably true (see *Origins & Destinations*, 1980). The snakes had once again triumphed over the ladders, and optimistic accounts of post-War reforms had to be severely revised for the reality of life. One of the more absurd examples of this policy was highlighted by Barnes & Lucas in their research on EPA schools in Inner London, where they showed that there were roughly equal numbers of 'disadvantaged and deprived' children in schools outside the EPA schools - as inside them!

In the early 1980s, the research baton was handed on in part *via* a programme 'Studies in Deprivation and Disadvantage', with funding from the Social Science Research Council and the Department of Health and Social Security. "Despite substantial economic advances and improved welfare services in Britain since the Second World War, there has been a conspicuous persistence of deprivation and maladjustment. In June 1972, Sir Keith Joseph, then Secretary of State for Social Services, drew attention to this. In particular, it seemed to him that social problems tended to recur in successive generations of the same families to form a 'cycle of deprivation'" - to quote from Muriel Brown and Nicola Madge (1982), who edited a series of thirteen books on (dysfunctional) families, poverty, health, and schooling-education. Brown and Madge provided a report on the series and the issue of transmitted deprivation with the title *Despite the Welfare State*, although some commentators might have suggested inserting the words 'and/or because of' somewhere in the title.

There are important links here with an enduring concern with communities, and I will return to these issues later, looking, for example, at the research and publications of the contemporaneous Community Development Projects.

So what role could, should, and do, schools play in the lives of children and young people today? In his 2006 book, *On Education,* Harry Brighouse alludes to this key issue by asking what it is for all of us to be a human being? If we can collectively decide, agree upon what are the virtues, best characteristics of the human condition, are we as a society, citizens, professionals and so on, providing the means whereby children and young people can accede to these criteria, these qualities? For example does the schooling of children and young people get in the way of their education? As I have suggested above, it is nothing new for children and young people to experience schooling as a set of 'hurdles', tests and exams, that are devised to 'sieve and grade', to domesticate, as well as liberate. To hold back, as well as promote. The familiar notions of sponsored- and contest-generated social mobility for children and young people still apply in an acutely stratified society (see my *Liberation & Domestication,* 2006). However, a crucial factor for many children and young people in contemporary Britain is that many of the traditional cultural-support mechanisms have been removed, and replaced by an open-ended, insatiable consumer culture, where the sky is the limit, and the gutter is an ever-likely repository. The acquisitive fist within the 'lifestyle' glove? And we are not merely considering cultural artefacts here, but crucially the values that are bound up in the presentational and representational package. Take, for example, the life of young people like me in the 1950s, where the door of cultural and social austerity had been pushed ajar by the resurgent economic and cultural liberalism of post-War reconstruction. I am reminded here of Vance Packard's dedication in his excellent 1960 book *The Waste Makers*: "To my Mother and Father who have never confused the possession of goods with the good life." For once that door *had* been pushed open, the fair and foul winds of American popular culture blew through our lives, and loves. The Cunard Yanks in Liverpool had their match in the south of England where teenagers had increasing access to the goods, and moral sensibilities, that appeared to be *déclassé*. At the beginning of the 1960s, my Art School was full of young people who wanted to be Beats. All right, we had to go to the local Co-op working men's outfitters to buy our Levi 501s, but even that added a certain *frisson* to the experience.

Were we then, or are now, capable of discriminating between the good, the bad, and the ugly? I realise some social theorists (usually referred to as post-modernists) would not concern themselves with these issues around action-taking as moral statements. But it worries me, it always has, and I shall return to address these concerns more fully.

Not all that long ago, and certainly within my lifetime, most people were supported in their everyday inter-relation with society and self by cultural groups in one guise or another. For example working class people had family, neighbourhood, workplace social groups, trades unions, co-operative and labour political institutions, religion and many other collective, mutual, groupings. Middle class people had some of these, especially family networks, and they also had professional associations that incorporated and protected them. Maintaining status differences all the time. These were what Raymond Williams (*q.v.*) referred to as 'knowable communities'. Known from within, but not always welcome of course, with sets of cultural rules that people might struggle against and attempt to renegotiate, developing their own style along the way. The experience of young people, women, and members of ethnic minorities are clear examples here. These 'knowable communities' were also recognised, and understood from without. For example *via* the stories and dramas that continued to reach a wider audience through television, cinema, Penguin books (which I look at briefly later on), and the like. Some academic writers in the 1970s-80s drew on this cultural creativity around ordinary people's everyday lives in developing their ideas about the nature and place of social class. Members of the Centre for Contemporary Cultural Studies at the University of Birmingham were one such group of researchers and theorists. Chas Critcher is a characteristic contributor, and in the book *Working Class Culture* that he co-edited with John Clarke and Richard Johnson, he sets out to establish the existence of a genre of writing that intentionally or otherwise crosses the boundaries between sociology, cultural studies, and history. 'There is no self-consciously interrelated tradition of sociological writing on working-class culture. In a sense, we have to construct a genre of working-class cultural studies' (1979). He then produces a list of studies that starts in 1956 with Dennis, Henriques and Slaughter's book *Coal is our Life* and ends with Roberts' *The Classic Slum*, and Frank Parkin's *Class Inequality and Political*

Order in 1971. Along the way, he incorporates Richard Hoggart, Raymond Williams and Edward Thompson. These last three are all outside of formal post-War British Sociology, while clearly making an enormous contribution to any sociological analysis of social class. Social theorists who were on the political (even Marxist) left drew on these diverse accounts and analyses of working class life to help emphasise the inherent contradictions of life in post War Britain. Many of these key social theorists were involved with adult education in a variety of ways: university extramural departments, WEA, TUC Education, Ruskin College, and so on. And may be this also reflects their self-imposed marginal status? (For an excellent account of these issues see Nick Stevenson's book *Culture, Ideology and Socialism: Raymond Williams and E.P.Thompson,* 1995).

I am looking at my review of *Working Class Culture* from September 1979, and what I noted with pleasure is the explicit aim of the writers to meld accounts of the collective with the biographic. This was not done in a romanticised or sentimental way, but genuinely trying to show the constant inter-relationships that take place between the personal and the public. You can take the person out of the culture, but can you take the culture out of the person? The novels, plays and poetry of Sillitoe, Storey, Barstow, Mercer, Potter, and Livings, *et al*, would suggest not. My own writing has always attempted to address the complex way in which we all reflect upon consciousness, and our conscious self, and seek to make sense of how other people are also doing this. Milan Kundera gets somewhere near the problem in his book *The Art of the Novel* (1986).

'A novel examines not reality but existence,
and existence is not what has occurred,
existence is the realm of human possibilities,
everything that man can become, everything
he's capable of. Novelists draw up a map of
existence by discovering this or that human
possibility. But again, to exist means: "being-
in-the-world". Thus both the character and
his world must be understood as
possibilities.'

A good deal of the most relevant and lasting accounts of
everyday life in post-War Britain assert precisely this point
about the range of possibilities available to people. Nor
should we forget the modernist and socialist project of
creating politically and culturally the ideal model for a new
kind of person. Not surprising, then, that so much of the
kind of writing identified by Critcher and others is resentful,
aspirational, fatalistic - and *optimistic*. They are culturally
creative responses in diverse forms, and during the years of
my childhood and teens, set within a context of social
democratic ideology and Welfare State growth. This context
included ideas about social justice and equity, and was
realised in both senses by the post-War settlement-type
agreements around access.

The real limits to a policy of 'just' providing a theoretical
access point for children of the working class was exposed
very early on in the post-War years, most punishingly by the
likes of Orwell in his dystopia *Nineteen Eighty-Four*. This was

a riposte to all that was 1948, the year that usually marks the creation of 'the Welfare State'. Orwell's forensic account sheet for post-War Britain drew attention to the triumph of a technically rational bureaucratic State that made a cultural virtue from using language as lies. Anyone interested in studying how cultural and political dominance, hegemony, can be delivered by a State apparatus in a 'beast and whore' relationship, with the available means of mass communication, should start with Orwell.

Other writers, like Michael Young went on to satirise the myth of meritocracy, and the relationship here with ideas and practice around access and choice. In the 1961 Pelican edition of *The Rise of the Meritocracy 1870-2033*, Young was speaking particularly, but not exclusively, about education, while also addressing wider concerns about welfare provision and equality. Young's argument was that this pursuit of the meritocratic ideal would lead to new and ever more entrenched elites rather than to equality. He foreshadowed the rise, and legitimation, of an individualism that provided the cultural context for a politics of selfishness. The privileges that 'meritocrats' considered to be rightfully theirs would then be passed on to their children by any appropriate means necessary. In a *Guardian* article on 30 June 2003, Young emphasised this point by reference to the (new) business elite: 'So assured have the elite become that there is almost no block on the rewards they arrogate to themselves. The old restraints of the business world have been lifted and, as the book also predicted, all manner of new ways for people to feather their own nests have been invented and exploited.'

Young's satire ended in 2033 with the rebellion of the lower orders. What year are we in now?

One of the key themes in this discussion of mine is to explore why and how the majority of people in post 1945 Britain were contributors to, and then victims of, a political culture that offered equality and democracy, and then delivered neither in any fundamental way.

In the last fifty years much has been made of 'the post-War settlement', the 'deal' struck between the interests of labour and the interests of capital, with (allegedly) the Labour government as honest broker, and legislator. But even here the measures taken though clearly beneficial to many, myself included, were arbitrary from the outset, primarily favoured the middle classes; and, even in fundamental ways, to whole systemic areas like social insurance, policies were devised around white working class men who were organised in trades unions.

Yes, of course, citizenship rights were in theory extended to all, and this was a functional need for post-War capitalism and State. Through a series of deals the Atlee government were able to draw up a framework for an incipient consensus politics, which sought to supplant the long-standing class war. 'Even then' a politics of selfishness was recognisable because the various deals, agreements, and accompanying legislation, did not make citizenship a reality for all. Look, for example, at the situation of women, working class young men, and, most distinctively, incoming ethnic minority migrants from 'the Empire'. Even the cultural speak of consensus politics could not disguise the whole swathes of inequality experienced in the reality of a continuing 'snakes and ladders' existence. Any ideas that the lowest-status workers may have harboured about a more convivial set of social relationships soon evaporated. Of course, there is an 'ideological smokescreen' that deflects criticism, and one manifestation of this phenomenon over many years has been setting the 'deserving poor' against their undeserving contemporaries. It could be argued that one outcome of this 'modern' social organization is the advent of *anomie*, the sociological theory that emphasises the social disequilibria created by the contradictions in social development. Anomie suggests two failings of the social forms that I have discussed. First, there is distributional arbitrariness, where there is unequal access to the 'opportunity structures' of contemporary society. Second, there is a regulative weakness in everyday life because the moral system is utilitarian in that it concentrates on *ends*, leaving the individual with only loose guidance as to the *means* of their actions to achieve these culturally valued ends. Ivan Illich emphasised this in his book, *Tools for Conviviality* (1973): 'In a consumer society there are inevitably two kinds of slaves: the prisoners of addiction and the prisoners of envy.' Values, aspiration, acquisitiveness, access, choice, and disappointment once again raise their heads.

Indeed, it is worth commenting on the current myth of choice at the point-of-access (to welfare needs provision). Neo-liberals seem to have forgotten that when people vote, they - the people - have already made those choices about access. They have looked at the political menu, and made their selections based on what might meet their needs. In view of the context of our political institutions, this is as near as we have got to democracy. So why then re-organise welfare provisions in a way that allegedly asks people to make those choices again in a 'supermarket' - like a goods-grasp that is profoundly *undemocratic?*

In the not too distant past, people not only recognised that they were individual human beings, they also understood they were *social* beings, and that they were not alone, abandoned, ideologically and politically cast adrift. They had the enduring safety of reciprocal relations. An aspect of the 'knowable community' was *trust*. By and large, people within their symbolically charged community and culture groupings regarded each other as peers, as people who did have collective experiences, long memories, and a sceptical (not cynical, yet) view of the various leaders. One of the triumphs of neo-liberalism has been to atomise people into *individuals* who are convinced that advancement is only possible through their own agency.

As I have suggested above, many of the dominating values of everyday life were conservative ones. In many respects life needed to change: for people to have more freedom, more agency, and an opportunity to set their own sights on a radical reorientation of their self within an increasingly technological, and media-driven, social comp-lexity. In the 1960s, there was much talk of affluence, 'never had it so good', 'we are all middle class now', and so on. One key dimension of these widely held ideas was the real standard of living, quality-of-life bonus people in general received from 'welfare state' provisions: care, services and benefits. Labour politicians usually referred to this largesse as 'the social wage', and much was made of the transformation of post-War British life from austerity to affluence.

But affluence was, is, a chimera; and, like poverty, affluence was, is, always relative. One key reason for this is that people's realisation of affluence was tied to rhetorically raised expectations allied to the acquisition of material goods by some sections of society previously denied them. Power and status differentials were not so amenable to change.

In any case, most people were not, are not, ready to be decanted from the relative safety of their traditional and supportive cultural groupings into a life, a world, where the signposts (let alone the goalposts) have been moved, abandoned, scrapped, re-branded, to be replaced by a consumer capitalism produced by a do-it-yourself, quick-fix guide on mental survival in an increasingly mad world. However, this one-size fits all acquisitiveness model does not work as a reasoned response to this cultural diaspora, and signs of alienation and anomie are all around us.

One familiar area of sociological theory that has sought to emphasise the value of the culturally collective is the concept of social capital.

> 'Its central thesis can be summed up in two words: relationships matter. By making connections with one another, and keeping them going over time, people are able to work together to achieve things that they either could not achieve by themselves, or

could only achieve with great difficulty.
People connect through a series of networks
and they tend to share common values with
other members of these networks; to the
extent that these networks constitute a
resource.'

                    - *Social Capital*, John Field (2003)

There are important links here with Williams' ideas on 'knowable communities', (see Williams' *The Country and the City*, 1985), and the wider discussion about the cultural (semi-) autonomy of people's lives when it comes to entering into democratic arrangements to address and resolve problems, and take actions that meet personal and collective needs.

Recent research in the East End of London (*The New East End*, Dench, Gavron and Young, 2006) emphasises just this point. The author's argue that the indigenous white working class feel let down by the very social welfare system that was supposed to make their lives better and more secure. Access to social housing is a key issue, and sections of the white population are resentful because they have 'lost out' to 'immigrant' families within the context of a contracting resource. This aspect of social welfare provision is precisely an example of top-down policy making, and delivery, of a crucial resource that excluded the clients from any effective decision-making. It epitomised the *undemocratic* nature of (at best, well meaning, often patronising) welfare provision.

Michael Collins touches on similar ground in his 2004 book *The Likes of Us: A Biography of the White Working Class*.

He relates the journey made by the white working class of south London from the sinned-against in a pre-Welfare State society to the lumpen, racist sinners in a multicultural Britain. Or at least that is the (convenient) label attached to this 'class' by the middle class media and attendant politicians, an aspect of the latter's social construction of a post-ideology Britain. This situation reminds me of the colonial era ethnographers-anthropologists who sat on their verandas and looked down on the exotic activities of the local savages. I am sure this is why we are subjected to so much 'reality' TV? It is also a further example of class being used as a negative appellation when it suits elites and their spokespersons to do so.

One of the real problems with a focus on the multicultural 'realities' as a 'litmus test' for the distinctive divisions in society, is that cultures are 'multi', and diverse, and so what? This is, in fact, another piece of the post-modern jigsaw that seeks to avoid reference to the economic class realities that blights everyday lives. The politico-media scene-setters would rather swap 'in the field' anecdotes about tribal variations as if that is what really divides people, as distinct from what unites them, oppression; compliments of modern, contemporary and ever more global capitalism.

While I was reading the recent East End research, focused as it is on a part of London, I was reminded of other places, and of Ken Coates and Richard Silburn's book, *Poverty: The Forgotten Englishmen*, first published as a Penguin Special (those good old days!) in 1970. Their study focused on the St. Ann's district in Nottingham. In that book, they asked questions about the continued existence of poverty in a land of plenty. They asked why it was possible for there to be such striking contrasts between the 'haves and the have nots' in 1960s Britain, and certainly after the election of the Wilson Labour Government in 1964.

Among others, they quote Aneurin Bevan on the disparity between the public and the private choices over quality of life expenditure. They emphasise the key issue of disposable income, and the rarely questioned, let alone challenged, right of the individual to make choices about the disposal of 'surplus' income. Coates and Silburn draw attention to the costs of these individual choices, both for the public purse, and other people without such disposable incomes. For example, to own and use a car seems to be a perfectly normal choice in our society. It is only in recent years that the real, and cumulative consequences, and costs, of those private actions have begun to be acknowledged. There has been ample discussion on the private control of public money (for example, Heclo & Wildasky, 1974), and in the increased privatisation of the 'public sector' of life has merely served to emphasise the truly undemocratic nature of decision-making in so many spheres of our everyday lives.

The concerns of Coates and Silburn, along with many similar commentators, reflect a more fundamental questioning of the so-called Welfare State - its nature, role, and outcomes. One of our finest post-War writers, Jeremy Seabrook, has characterised these changes in the lives of working class communities:

'When we talk about the resources of the

poor - the human abilities which evolved to
cope with a dearth of material things - we are
talking of real, substantial skills. These have
traditionally been so much part of the daily
life of working class communities that no one
commented upon them until they seemed,
suddenly, close to extinction.'

- 'The Great Consumer Swindle', *The
Guardian*, 21 August 1982

Seabrook goes on to make the point that the Market,
aided and abetted by all post-War governments, has
inveigled working people in to reorienting the values that
guide their understanding of everyday life. What matters,
what counts, in terms of status, is *who to look to*.

Or, as Ivan Illich put it: 'Man must choose whether to be
rich in things or in the freedom to use them.' (*Deschooling
Society, 1971*). Richard Hoggart in his 1957 book *The Uses of
Literacy* comments similarly on how sensible people's heads
were turned by the impact of market-generated, and profit-
focused popular cultures.

Richard Sennett, the American Sociologist, who has spent
many years working in Britain, made similar points in his
1998 book *The Corrosion of Character*. Sennett subtitles this
critique 'the personal consequences of work in the new
capitalism', and seeks to explore the ways in which people
who thought they were competent, skilled, and functioning
appropriately, are rendered inadequate, or harbour strong
feelings of inadequacy, by new sets of criteria over which

they have had no say or control. Many professional practitioners in Britain have articulated just such a malaise, where their very vocational commitment to a set of values in service has been under siege from a 'new' managerialism and a regimen of bean counters (see my 2006 publication *Professionalism & Practice'* for a lengthier discussion).

At the time of writing, I am looking at coverage in *The Guardian* of the fortieth anniversary of the screening of *Cathy Come Home* on TV.

Written by Jeremy Sandford, and made by Ken Loach and Tony Garnett, this BBC film was watched by 11.8 million people in 1966. It created an enormous, and generally shocked, response from the audience and Parliament, and led to the creation of SHELTER, the homelessness-housing policy pressure group. We should not be too surprised by the size of the audience for this production because this was a 'golden age' for TV docu-dramas, and current affairs. Both the BBC and ITV were at the top of their game in providing a wealth of educational, informative, and entertaining films for an enthusiastic audience.

What is also worth noting is what has happened in the forty years since its first screening. According to Shelter, 'the number of households in temporary accommodation has soared from 64,000 in 1976 to 100,000 today. The building of social housing has fallen by 87 per cent over the same period...In the year that *Cathy Come Home* was first broadcast, the government built 180,000 houses compared with 20,000 last year.' (*Guardian* 15/2/06.) I would add here that *the* photograph of 'Cathy' in her buttoned-up against the travails of life coat has become an icon of all that went wrong in the 1960s.

The sell-off of council houses, a Labour-to-Tory-to-New Labour strategy, has chimed with the obsession with home 'ownership', and should remind us just how much successive governments have easily acceded to, indeed actively reproduced, a politics of selfishness.

Very soon after New Labour came to office in May 1997 the Social Exclusion Unit (SEU) was established within the Cabinet Office. Its aims reflected several complex issues concerning the State apparatus; increasing voter indifference in poor areas, and a lack of interest in the niceties of citizenship, high incidence of deviance and crime among the working classes and within working class neighbourhoods, persistent racism (including institutional racism within key organizations), school and schooling failures, and so on, and so on. These are the kind of complex and multifaceted 'social problems' that any new government ministers will find landed on their desk. (Or in their red box, of course, to keep them snowed under!)

They are, have been increasingly, the interminable, intransigent issues that dog every administration. The Home Office (the Ministry of the Interior) responsible as it is for the maintenance of Civil Society has maintained a consistent portfolio for such matters. The 'Ship of State' cannot be allowed to be so buffeted by the enduring storms that are the manifestations of profound social injustice and marginalisation that it might sink! The 'balance' in the body politic must be maintained where and whenever possible. Potential dissident tribes must be courted, even cajoled, in to some form of assimilation. The *appearance* of consensus, social harmony and peaceful coexistence is crucial if the always-enthusiastic middle class voters are to be kept happy. Utilitarianism reigns supreme with policies that seek to create the illusion of order and security in the face of the chaos and risk caused by roulette capitalism, and sponsored acquisitiveness.

The zealous advocates of 'monetarist' economic policy entertained no such niceties in their 1960s onwards fight to the death with the Keynesians in all political parties.

As always with the election of a 'Labour' government the situation is somewhat different. The labour constituency invests a good deal of moral outrage and ethical concern into such administrations. 1997 was no exception, and even though many sensible and experienced people knew that 'baton' Blair and his associates were not even social democrats, but the inheritors of Thatcher's legacy, expectations still ran high. Many well-meaning people in the new administration were happy to be associated with measures for civic renewal, for schemes that would seek to get the increasingly dispossessed working class re-included in the great British scheme of things. Vast amounts of time and effort were spent on the SEU and the neighbourhood renewal 'project', and like many people I have boxes full of the well-argued outpourings from those early years. Either side of '97 Blair had even made forays into debates about 'Community', and its central importance in our everyday lives. He even joined forces with the American social theorist Etzioni to make some very obvious and non-controversial comments about the value of community in terms of social bonds and shared goals.

Nine years on we have had David Miliband as minister for communities addressing precisely the same issues, sifting through identical mountains of paper, exhorting people to take all this 'active citizenship' stuff seriously. But, of course, there is nothing new here, and one cannot help thinking that Marx's dictum about history repeating itself, first time as tragedy, and second time as farce, is apposite for young Milliband. And given who his father was, he should know. We have been here before, with one of the most recent incarnations of this phenomenon being the 'Urban Programme's Community Development Projects' of the 1970s.

'The original brief of the Community Development Programme rested on some dubious assumptions. Poverty, bad housing, and so on, were, it was implied, residual flaws in a society that had solved all of its basic problems. There was also the "blame the victim" element in the Programme's conception: poverty and deprivation were allegedly the fault of individuals, as well as "deprived areas" - or places where there happened to be particular concentrations of people with the special characteristics that made them poverty-prone. The solutions then were supposed to lie in self-help by the poor.' (*The Costs of Industrial Change*, CDP, 1977).

The Home Office within the 1974 Wilson government had identified twelve 'neighbourhood-based experiments' across Britain's (already existing) industrial wasteland. In 1974 the CDP collective released *Jobs in Jeopardy*, which emphasised as much: 'Without a sound economic base a community cannot survive.' The 1977 publication concluded with arguing that endless 'regeneration' tinkering would not resolve the inherent situations identified, and should be replaced by 'measures designed to control the activities of capital.'

There was not much hope of this, then, when Margaret Thatcher was elected in 1979 on a programme of re-capitalising capitalism, increasingly denuding the already-cut public purse, and linked to a direct confrontation with organised labour and the further immiserisation of the marginalised.

By 1997 'New Labour' had either marginalised or expelled those voices that would put debate about the issue of the forces and relations of capital onto the agenda of change. In an early example of the new-broom triumphalist bandwagon that was New Labour, Clause 4 was abolished.

There are many fundamental issues here about democratic values, or the lack of them, and about the misunderstanding of the nature of the State and the symbiotic relationship between State and (consumer) capitalism.

There is a long history of social democratic-Labour Party politicians (of all kinds) wanting to take over the management of the State as a way to administer their often well-meaning ideas in to practice. One key factor here is that nearly all these politicians are also committed to the maintenance of capitalism as their preferred economic system. Of course, many such politicians have advocated a capitalism 'with a human face' - some hope. Even in the immediate post-War period, there was significant agreement among the three main political parties on the necessity to shore-up a battered and ailing capitalism. Money was spent on a massive investment in public utilities, and other aspects of infrastructure needs, like a social insurance scheme, health care, schooling, and so on. The labouring classes were persuaded to 'sign up' to this strategy, to throw in their lot with a succession of governments who were essentially offering the same vision of a renewed or new Britain. This vision encompassed some redistribution of the 'goodies', a few more 'doors' prised open to allow access, and a greater emphasis on the 'ladders' rather than the 'snakes' of everyday life. In this post-War 'brave new world' there was very little exploration of transforming Britain *via* the establishment of a democratic socialism. Many Labour Party supporters (and others as well) fail to understand the nature of the State, run as it is in the interests of the owning and ruling classes. Over the years, many supporters, and thereby voters, have believed that conference decisions, manifesto promises, and personal pledges by senior members and leaders of the Party made in opposition will be kept to when in government. How many times do people need to have demonstrated to them that this is simply not going to happen, because once these politicians have got their hands on the controls of 'the ship of State' the realities of the system take over. Once in office (or invariably well before) successive generations of Labour Governments are told what they can and cannot do. They have been permitted to do certain things, usually measures that will enhance the functioning of the capitalist economy, maintain the privileges of the well-to-do, and deal with the occasional irate demands of the working class, born as it is out of frustration, disappointment, and a sense of sheer injustice.

I recall very well the ideas circulating in the Labour movement prior to the 1964 General Election. Wilson & Co. had given the failing Tories a very hard time in Parliament, and Wilson in particular had made a specific issue of utilising new technologies linked to economic planning. When in Government, they created the Department of Economic Affairs (DEA) with the explicit aim of wresting from the Treasury the apparatus of long-term planning. George Brown was the Secretary of State at the DEA, and a good deal was made of the new National Plan complete as it was with generous growth targets and the like. However, the DEA did not last long, the Plan was shelved, George Brown was moved, and Treasury orthodoxies reinstated for all to see. It is a sociological truism that power can only be understood in the close observation of its manifestation in the everyday relations of society. The power that H.M. Treasury has held over successive governments is one such example, apparent through the symbiotic inter-relations between the interests of capitalism both outside, and inside, of government. The very fluidity of personnel movements between the State apparatus and the City of London emphasises the harmony of interests and aims.

All these examples discussed above should remind us that politics is supposed to be the alternative to war, in this case, class war. However, if people, individually and collectively, are consistently let down by a (party) politics that is allegedly secular, civilised, humane and democratic, they may well turn elsewhere for solutions to their problems. They may even turn to, and embrace, a belief that the Gods will intervene on their behalf, or even worse, to fascist promises. There is now, once again, the suggestion that there is a 'crisis of legitimacy', that people have loosened, even broken, their (social) bond with liberal democracy, and representative party politics. And this is periodically an issue that the governing party has to deal with in its management of the State apparatus. At least once a decade there is a reoccurrence of this 'crisis', and it is a serious matter because authority = power + legitimation, and if the last of these goes missing the exercise of power is increasingly seen as unacceptable.

There is a widespread sense, or feeling, among citizens of disenfranchisement. People regularly say to me, Who can I vote for? Questions are being raised about the real extent of a meaningful, transparent and realisable democracy in society. People are aware that democracy is an active process; they want to engage with these political relations, being 'grass-roots', organic, rather than external forces and instruments that dominate their lives. Henri Lefebvre summed this up well in the mid-1960s: "According to Marx, there is no such thing as 'true democracy'. For him, the sense of democracy is that it discloses the truth of politics. He sees it not as a system, but as a process, which comes down essentially to a struggle for democracy. The latter is never completed because democracy can always be carried forward - or forced back. The purpose of the struggle is to go beyond democracy, and beyond the democratic state, to build a society without state power." (Lefebvre, 68).

Nor should we underestimate the view that human beings have lost faith in themselves as a morally viable species, an aspect of "western civilization's estrangement from its humanity". Frank Ferudi (2006) argues that 'the new misanthropy' is widespread, and that a genuine sense of apocalyptic doom has gripped many thinkers. He suggests that the time is right for a 'renewing our faith in people' kind of approach to addressing the current, not far from new, contradictions in many people benefiting from the products of a globalized super-abundance. Some agency, yes, but invariably making the wrong choices.

I say 'far from new' because once again we find Marx discussing precisely these issues, and offering up the stark 'choice' of communism or barbarism.

One way in which we know about all these concerns about our contemporary situation and future prospects is *via* the media's everyday outpourings, so much of which is not only money-profit driven, but banal and vulgar into the bargain. The abuse of such sophisticated technologies puts our cultures into 'negative equity'.

> 'Never before in human history has so much cleverness been used to such stupid ends. The cleverness is in the creation and manipulation of markets, media and power; the stupid ends are in the destruction of community, responsibility, morality, art, religion, and the natural world.'

This is Ivo Mosley in *Dumbing Down: culture politics and the Mass Media* (2000). I am reminded that this kind of criticism is not new, recalling, for example, that Bertolt

Brecht once referred to (Hollywood) commercial movies as 'laxatives of the soul'.

So, now, taking up Mosley's argument, we need to ask ourselves some searching questions about how, and why, the media has got into the all-powerful position it has in contemporary life. Is one of the real reasons why it matters because so many otherwise apparently sensible people believe so much of what they see and hear?

With these concerns in mind, let us return to the key ideas of ideology and hegemony, and explore the meanings and usage of these concepts.

Anyone who points to the detrimental effects of the media and other culture industries must justify their claim. Most theorists turn to both ideology and hegemony to develop their argument.

My definition of ideology is similar to many others in that I want to assert that ideologies are clusters of ideas, images, and assumptions, by which people make sense of their social world. These ideologies seem to make social identities clear, and serve to legitimate the power relations in our everyday lives. Common-sense explanations of phenomena (events-actions) prevail, unquestioned, un-challenged. We might feel that something like ideology exists in society, but this is 'what other people do'. For example, the stock cynicism about propaganda emanating from politicians. This is usually referred to as a 'restricted' view of ideology, and is distinguished from a 'relaxed' view of ideology, where we subscribe to the view that everyone is an ideologist. We are all trying to impose *our* interpretation of everyday life. It could be argued that this second definition demonstrates that at least people are aware of the way in which ideas and images are, or could be, manipulated, and managed to achieve, to meet, someone's desired ends? People are increasingly aware of the role of advertising, and how clever and entertaining devices are used to capture attention and interest. There is a raised consciousness about the role of advertisers to flatter, frighten, cajole, amuse us, and generally 'pull our strings'.

Any discussion about these aspects of our everyday lives must acknowledge the 'sieve of the self' that such information passes through. We do place meanings upon what we see, *etcetera*, with interpretations made on the basis of our past experience of such things. A crucial aspect of understanding the nature of the self here is the concept of role.

> 'By choosing social role as a major concept we are able to reconstruct the inner experience of the person as well as the institutions which make up an historical social structure. For man as a person…is composed of the specific roles that he enacts, and the effects of enacting these roles upon himself. And society as a *social structure* is composed of roles as segments variously combined in its total circle of institutions. The organisation of roles is important in building up a particular social structure; it also has psychological implications for the persons who act out the social structure.'

> - C. Wright Mills and Hans Gerth, 1954

So, according to Mills and Gerth, we are all 'Janus-like', facing in two directions at the same time: the private and the public, self and society, citizens and State, producer and consumer, mind and ideology. Several years ago, I tried to think my way through some of these complexities about the *structures* of the media and culture industry, and ourselves as choice-makers, as people with agency. I started from the fundamental maxim that we are all action takers, but not necessarily in conditions of our choosing. But I also wanted to show that we could not assume, just because the outcome of people taking action was, for example, the consumption of some particular thing, that this was entirely their own choice. As Vance Packard once said there are *'hidden* persuaders', and we need to flush them out, to lay bare what it is these people are up to and why, what motivates them? As work in progress, I came up with the concept of Ideological Cultural Apparatuses (ICAs), which sought to link together the ideology issues with the realm of the cultural in our lives, including the media. But I also wanted to link these with the notion of organic structures, institutions, individuals and groups with a range of motives to pursue a technology for the manipulation of hearts and minds. (For more on ICAs, see my essay 'Transformations' in *Liberation & Domestication,* 2006).

This in turn brings me to hegemony. As with ideology, it is not my intention to provide an extensive discussion of this concept, rather my aim is to demonstrate why it has been of use to me. Essentially, hegemony is about both domination and leadership. Hegemonism as a concept was used by the likes of Mao Tse-tung to describe a cultural version of imperialism. This is much in the same way that many writers have suggested that working class (creative) cultures have been colonised by the dominant economic class; hijacked, repackaged, glamorised, and sold back to the very same people at a profit. This version of hegemony suggests that the ruling class/elites in any society have maintained their ownership and control of the cultural apparatuses. This sense of culture would be broad enough to encompass schooling, means of information exchange, control of the 'air-waves', and so on, as well as the media and other standard culture industries. This use of hegemony suggests that the very manner in how most people gather and exchange information and knowledge (even about them-selves) is managed and orchestrated by those with vast amounts of power and control over our everyday lives. These processes are deliberate and exploitative, actively seeking to maintain and develop a complex set of structures that directly reproduce the oppression of the many by the few. Through the manipulation of culture and politics those with power do not always have to resort to armed means to protect and promote their privileges.

A second sense of hegemony has derived largely from Lenin, and, importantly, from Gramsci, in the early twen-tieth century. This sense of the concept emphasises the need for the intellectual, cultural and political forces of opposition to combine in challenging the 'cultural' dominance of the ruling class. This system of alliances work out and deploy the means whereby the regular duping of the people can be challenged and stopped. The nefarious activities of the rulers and controllers must be exposed for what they are:

selfish, greedy, short-sighted, and so on.

A crucial element of this challenge to oppressors is the goal of a genuine democratic socialism: bringing together the common ownership of the wealth-creating resources in society, through the processes of inclusive decision- making; and returning the collective ownership of labour to people; with means of discussing the appropriate ways in which human labour can be used to meet the needs of all.

So, the aim of this brief excursion into theory is to demonstrate why the struggle for democratic cultural values is a *struggle* - and why we need to engage in that struggle.

A further, related aspect to these contexts is for me to explain what I mean by democratic values, and democratic *cultural* values.

First and foremost, democratic values are those that put democratic relations at the top of our social agendas. Of course there remains a diverse range of definitions of democracy, could it realistically be otherwise? Many people feel that the goal of a true democracy is this: a multi-party representative parliamentary system, with a fully en-franchised population, within certain agreed guidelines, one person one vote, with choice. This fits with the 'liberal democracy' of most modern societies. However, the former Soviet Union was a good example of where some people claimed that in a one-party state most of the criteria above still applied. There have been other variations on these themes, which I leave the reader to explore. One of the recent issues in Britain has been around the actual role and influence of opposition parties. Since the election of Blair & Co. in 1997, it has been argued that, given New Labour's majority, and the weakness of the other political parties, we do, in effect, live in a one-party state. This line of argument does not only raise questions about the opposition parties, it also focuses attention on the nature and role of the Parliamentary Labour Party (PLP). How effective is the PLP in regulating and trimming the activities of the Executive? Does the role of backbenchers in Parliament on select committees give us cause for hope? Are most of the PLP merely 'lobby fodder'? And, if they are, is this because as professional politicians they are all desperate to keep their jobs and careers? Most of the 'old guard' in the PLP have tended to become members of the 'awkward squad' that regularly 'sounds-off' about the excesses of Blair & Co (or, as this is published, Brown & Co.)? This can make for temporary entertainment, but we should remember that most of these 'old Labour' stalwarts were on the right of the Labour Party, and actively involved in the various witch-hunts to expose and expel any left-wing and Marxist members. This task, having been completed under Kinnock's watch, left the field clear for the rag, tag and bobtail of SDP, Tory defectors, and neo-liberals like Blair and Mandelson, to move in and take over unopposed. As Tony Benn has often pointed out the dominant tendency in the PLP has been social democratic (at best) and not democratic socialist. As I have discussed above, the former were always happy to enter in to deals with the capitalist class around State funding and compensatory welfare, believing, as they did, and do, that concessions can be wrung from the privileged and powerful. Management of the State apparatus by such governments invariably plays into the hands, and does the daily bidding of, the real ruling class.

Democratic socialists have generally argued that without the social ownership of the economy, and the wholesale empowerment of all people through a genuinely representative system of decision-making in society, there will be no fundamental change in inequality and injustice.

As I have discussed earlier, it is clear that the culture industries in general, and the media in particular, play a crucial role in the maintenance of a society where inequality, injustice, and privilege are reproduced on a daily basis. The media tends to represent, and reproduce, dominant values that serve to maintain the *status quo* of unequal power relations in our everyday lives. The media influence, of course, is not all one-way-traffic, and people of diverse cultural kinds place a range of meanings on the their lives, and the world around them. However, the dominance of consumer capitalism, neo-liberal rhetoric on individualism and choice, and the real lack of access that most people have to decision-making, is anti-pathetic to an active democracy. Indeed, the current crisis of disengagement from the conventional political processes, and a pervasive sense of disenfranchisement among many people, has once again thrown the State 'managers' in to a panic. We are once again witnessing a flurry of activity around 'active citizenship', and 'community spirit regeneration'. However, if we consider this rhetoric for a few minutes, it is easy to detect the hypocrisy, for example, with regard to the State maintaining both strategic control and infrastructure investment. Young people, as usual, are good exemplars of

State double-speak. On the one hand, young people are experiencing more and more social control *via* ASBOs, welfare to work schemes, lack of choice in schooling, and so on, while being exhorted to do even more voluntary work in their local community. Even apparently progressive welfare policy still carries traces of the conventional care-and-control approach to provision.

So, what is going on *culturally*? Ideas, images, hearts and minds 'stuff', directly influences how we perceive, understand, and respond to discussions about how best to organize society for the benefit of all.

The role of intellectuals is often cited in discussions about hegemony, and the struggle to open up the means of communication, to allow ideas and options to be debated. Cultural historians, like Stefan Collini, have addressed these issues (see Collini's *Absent Minds*) attempting to both define the characteristics of 'the intellectual', and clarify the role occupied by such persons. There is certainly a long history of a perverse British reluctance to acknowledge the existence of 'intellectuals' or embrace their positive role in the life of society. There is a pervasive sense that all this intellectual 'stuff' is something that Continentals engage in, but not pragmatic down-to-earth Anglo-Saxons. Is this arcane theory of inscrutable theorists just another version of the Norman Yoke? This negative, and primarily politically right wing, social construction of scholarship and intellectuals merely serves to reinforce the stereotypes and prejudices that close-off ideas and discussion. Intellectuals need, and are defined in, their cultural role by 'publics'. The genuinely authoritative voice *is* needed in everyday discourse to allow for a range of informed and speculative options and alternatives to be posed. Intellectuals, and certainly academics, must write for, and talk to, a wide(ning) audience, applying their ideas to practical solutions. Questions need to be asked, 'conventional wisdoms' need to be challenged; politicians and their acolytes should be required to place their evidence within an open and transparent process of debate. Public discourse needs to be developed in ways that convey 'ownership' to as diverse a population as effective communications will allow. The nature, role, and democratisation of new and old technologies are key issues here. This evokes the role of political theatre, TV drama, an investigative press, 'public' art, satire in diverse forms, internet based information and argument, risk taking publishers, inventive and engaging 'world' music, and myriad cultural forms.

These 'practical' concerns should never be far from our explorations of how best to think critically, and act collectively, in the interests of everyone.

This is, for example, why *education* in all its forms is so vital, and why it remains a source of hope and optimism despite all the attempts by New Labour and other conservatives to curtail its capacity to enlighten and revitalise the struggle against the dead hand of instrumental reason.

It is also important to say that the media along with education should not just be giving people what they 'want', but making available what they did not know that they needed.

So, in conclusion, let me just add that one reason for

discussing these issues is to emphasise the importance of looking at, reflecting upon, and learning from good examples of what worked in the past. Without being over-philosophical, it is always worth remembering just how close to us (individually and collectively) and relevant are aspects of 'the past' to our understanding of the present. We are, of course, being selective in focusing on specific cultural phenomena (because it suits our argument to do so). However, we would hope to justify this methodology on the ground that it is all too easy to overlook what works well in the discourses of, and for, a more democratic life. It has been very convenient for the new authoritarians to banish these 'pasts' and 'presents' to the same dustbin that 'history' went in to.

Simon Schama concludes his epic BBC *History of Britain* (2006) by turning to George Orwell's *Nineteen Eighty-Four*:

> "History and memory are not the antithesis
> to free will, but the condition of it. When
> O'Brien, the arch-deceiver who has
> persuaded Winston Smith that he is running
> a resistance group suggests sealing his
> recruitment with a toast to the future,
> Winston lifts his glass and drinks instead:
>   'To the past.'
>   'The past is more important," agreed
> O'Brien gravely.'
> And, of course, for the reason that history is
> the enemy of tyranny, oblivion is its greatest
> accomplice. By encouraging forgetfulness,

the Party became free to impose on its
hapless subjects its own version of whatever
past it chose."
        - quoted by Simon Schama, BBC (2006).

Why are we regularly presented with TV and cinema filmic versions of dystopias as distinct from some creative accounts of alternative outcomes for human society? Why not sit down to watch an adaptation of William Morris' *News from Nowhere*, rather than yet another representation of our collective future as 'anarchic', brutal and short?

So, we do need to acknowledge those 'knowable communities' that could feed in to an optimistic portrayal of our futures. Our current situation, in Britain as elsewhere, is not 'the end of history', nor the much earlier predicted 'end of ideology'. Recognising and realising our human potentials can help us to find ways of reinventing these more democratic cultures in ways that meet our current and future needs.

Penguins and Pelicans

I do not actually know how many Penguins and Pelicans surround me as I write. Even though I have never felt moved to count them, I realise that there are a lot of them. Indeed I have already made reference to several of them in what I have written above. I would suggest that I am certainly not alone in having many of these books by me, nor is it so surprising that someone of my age, interests, and vocation should have accumulated these worthy texts. In his 2005 biography of Allen Lane (*The Life and Times of Allen Lane*) the founder of Penguin, Jeremy Lewis emphasises the particular appeal of these books. They successfully brought to a large and expanding audience books that were inexpensive, portable, thought provoking, and erudite. The first ten paperbacks appeared in 1935, and at six old pence cost the equivalent of a packet of cigarettes. In a stroke, Penguins and then Pelicans democratised the marketplace of books, and contributed more than anything else at the time to the expansion of the English common reader. Lewis like other commentators on Lane has made the point that the latter was not a 'bookish' man. We might assume that Lane's empathy with the common reader was a key factor in his strategy for Penguin. The books were also, essentially, educational, and fitted well into a culture of left-leaning, *free thought*-inspired, self-help. Indeed, there is clear evidence of an atavistic character of the 'new reader', linked with the politically oriented, secular, republican, and freethinking tradition of the late-eighteenth and nineteenth centuries.

Lewis mentions the Workers' Educational Association

(WEA) as one of the important links: '...the WEA was a fine embodiment of the earnest, nonconformist, self-improving tradition that had inspired J.M.Dent to found Everyman's Library.' (Lewis 2005.)

I recall being absorbed by my first Pelicans, pleased to have them in my hand or pocket, in the same way I cherished my LPs of Vaughan Williams, Holst, and Bach. This was all education without any semblance of schooling, spirituality without any reference to religion, and patriotism without being a flag-waving, jingoistic, monarchist!

In the opening essay, I have already made reference to Penguin Education books. In addition to numerous books about education and schooling, Penguin education created a whole range of texts that were subject-specific. For example, there were Penguin modern sociology Readings, and series of titles: *Social Inequality* (1969), *Sociology of Law* (1969), *Kinship* (1971), *Political Sociology* (1971), *Sociology of the Family* (1971), and so on. These texts were an invaluable source for students, teachers, and the general reader.

> "Penguin Modern Sociology offers essential Readings over the whole range of thinking and research, both classical and contemporary, in sociology and social anthropology. The distinguished Advisory Board is international in composition, and this is reflected in the individual books, which are edited by leading authorities and contain, in many cases, material receiving its first translation into English."

And even though this is a back-cover promotional pitch by the publishers, it was true.

I mentioned above that Lane was not a 'bookish' man himself, but he employed and/or collaborated with plenty of them. Indeed, as the years went by and the firm expanded considerably, I have a sense that many members of the 'bookish establishment' moved in to positions of control, and were fairly conservative in their attitudes to changes in house style.

An example of these tensions is in the appointment of the designer Germano Facetti in 1960. In his *Guardian* obituary of Facetti on April 11 2006, Richard Hollis commented on his historic appointment: 'Lane hired Facetti to bring Penguin covers up to date. Facetti introduced young designers and, beginning with the crime series in 1962, slowly re-made Penguin's identity. Many of the covers he designed himself, aiming to provide 'a visual frame of reference to the work of literature as an additional service to the reader.'" It is clear that Facetti brought his cultural values with him; these had been developed over the post-War years in an eclectic range of roles. Facetti worked with Ernesto Rogers (the grandfather of Richard Rogers) on the journal *Domus*, where the artistic programme was to: "educate in aesthetic judgement, in technical skills and ethical attitudes, all three directed to the same purpose, namely building a society".

And so, Penguins and Pelicans find themselves a place among the Herbivores.

New Society

I was a fan of *New Society* (1962–1988) even before I started teaching Sociology full-time in 1973. As a teacher, I found the weekly magazine invaluable, a view shared by everyone I knew in the world of social sciences, teachers or otherwise. The regular mix of news, feature articles, research updates, book reviews, education-focused adverts, and so on, became addictive and indispensable. In the later years of the magazine, its value to teachers of social science studies increased with the addition of 'pull-out' supplements on topical issues like 'The Community', or key theorists like 'Mead'. This kind of teaching support material, called *Society Today,* was moved around the magazine in later years, but the concept remained the same until 1988. The editorial team also produced collections of articles brought together under themes like 'Education'. These were available by post, and were ideal source material for teachers and researchers. *New Society* was merged with *New Statesman* in 1988 with promises that it would retain its special voice, but it never recovered, and we all knew it was the parting of a much-revered ally.

It would be impossible to render a full account of *New Society* in the paragraphs I have allocated, but what I hope to do is reflect the value of the magazine within the general context set above. I have therefore decided to consider the first edition, some from 1978-9, and another small batch from 1987-88. My reasoning here is that this will give a flavour of both continuity and change in *New Society*, and how this reflected upon change and continuity in British society at that time.

The first edition of *New Society* appeared on Thursday, 4 October 1962 at a cost of one shilling. It was born out of the success of the *New Scientist* (launched in 1956), and indeed one of the arguments put forward for creating *New Society* was the hope to replicate the value to the scientific community that *New Scientist* had been. The first editor was Timothy Raison, and from the outset the magazine's format was that of an eclectic and enlightening mixture. In this first edition, there were articles by Barbara Wootton ("Socrates, Science and Social Problems"), Edmund Leach ("Beasts and Triangles"), and T.H. Marshall ("World Congress of Sociology"). Timothy Raison interviewed Henry Brooke, the new Home Secretary, with the latter contributing the following gem: "When I went to the Home Office in July, it was entirely new to me. I quickly received a deep impression of more personal and individual work than anything I had done before. The tradition of the Home Office is that the Home Secretary and the people at the top find time to bring their brains to bear on the individual case, for instance, a deportation order. It was a sharp change from the Treasury, where I was dealing with facts and figures." (*NS*, Vol. 1, No.1 1962). The Prime Minister of the day was, of course, Harold Macmillan.

In his lengthy first editorial, Raison set out the aim of the magazine to reflect the 'chaos and movement' of the times. He argued that there was a climate of uncertainty in British society, and how prescient that was to be. He reflected upon the post-War success of the natural and physical sciences to attract good minds, research funding, and kudos for expanding bodies of knowledge; all of this, in a practical, problem-solving way. Raison argued that it was now the well overdue turn of the social sciences to follow suit. He suggested that public sector funding for research will only come with a clear demonstration of a practical policy oriented role, coupled with a pragmatic approach to ideas:

> "Luckily for British social scientists, they stem from a tradition which is dominated by the pragmatic rather than the theoretical: they would be likely to find support still harder to come by if they were the heirs of Weber, say, rather than of Booth and the Webbs.

> "*New Society* will share in all this. We shall not ignore ideas and theories: indeed, we shall see their interpretation as one of the principal challenges to us. But we aim above all to link the study of society with practice: to tell the manager what the psychologist has to say, to make the town planner aware of what the social anthropologist is revealing, to inform the local government official or councillor of the trends revealed by the demographer…The experience of the practitioner and the research of the academic are complementary, and our contributors will be drawn from both groups."

> - *N.S.*

And so it proved for the next twenty-six years.

One significant bonus of reading *New Society* over these years lay in the editorial team's determination to attract some of the best writers of the time. People who really did reflect and address the *zeitgeist*. For example I mentioned above the collections of articles put together, and can recall how Basil Bernstein took centre stage in the one devoted to 'Education', perhaps most famously his article "Education Cannot compensate for Society". Edward Thompson was another regular contributor; this being the opening of his 19 October 1978 article "The State versus its 'Enemies'":

"Let us consider State Trials. I cannot say why these should come into my mind this month, unless it may be that it is in the midst of general public silence that a historian is best able to meditate."

Of course Thompson was meditating on, and went on to write about, the role of Samuel Silkin, the Labour Government Attorney-General in *the* Official Secrets issue of the day, the Aubrey-Berry-Campbell case. Thompson argues that there seems to be little or no interest in the country for the historical role of 'state trials', and key issues of the selection, vetting, and role of juries. British citizens seem to be suffering more from *ennui* than *ire*? Thompson goes on to suggest that perhaps one solution to counteract this 'boredom' would be to turn the whole history of state trials in to a tourist attraction, anticipating, of course, the huge growth the heritage industry. Thompson ends his piece thus: "My subject has been the antique customs of yester-year. I find, on a review of the press, that the subject excites only boredom. I do not know where in all England I could place this piece, save that the Editor of this journal bears me an old friendship. He is too soft-hearted a fellow to see me, in my dotage, turned away…"

I can recall discussing with friends, on both sides of 1979, the strange case of those on the Left having to defend the ancient traditions of British citizenry, attempting to stand in the way of the surge of the neo-liberal changes to our lives and liberty.

Another writer that regularly graced the pages of *New Society* at this time, and later, was Jeremy Seabrook, a true heir to Orwell. In his article of 20 May 1988 'Waging War on the Poor', he argues that ". . .the poor, rather than being filled with envy of the rich, admire them their wealth. But the rich, it seems, hate the poor." He concludes the article in his characteristic way: "The decline of class consciousness, like the attenuation of many alleged evils, is not quite the unalloyed good that might have been anticipated, for so many other kinds of consciousness seem to have decayed with it. Indeed, conscience itself appears to have been one of the principal casualties. Certainly, the vision of a society without conflict in its universal deference to the curiously levelling monoculture of money is calculated to lift the hearts of the rich; but it may be that the noisy champagne celebrations over the reduction to impotence of the Labour movement and the demise of Socialism are both in-appropriate, and perhaps premature."

While writing this, the image of Harry Enfield's character 'LoadsaMoney' comes to mind, along with the joys of watching *Spitting Image* on ITV.

A regular feature of *New Society* was an 'Arts in Society'

section, and I am now looking at an article by John Berger, a regular contributor to these pages. This piece on 'Alternative Photography' is from 24 August 1978, and begins and ends with a celebration of Susan Sontag's *On Photography*. Berger opens by commenting that: "These essays allow us to see the extent to which our culture and our economic system depend upon the use of cameras so that photographed images are continually inserted between experience and reality." Berger notes Sontag's argument that the camera serves the interests of capitalism *via* "spectacle" for the masses, and surveillance, for the rulers, and presses on to question whether an alternative photographic practice is possible? Berger draws a distinction between the private photograph, which is likely to be directly related to personal memory and meaning, and the public photograph, which is essentially 'context-less'. Any use can be made of the public photograph because it has been rendered 'dead' and there-fore lends itself to arbitrary use. I have always felt much the same about popular and pop music, where people like John Street and Simon Frith have argued that once an iconoclastic Rock 'n' Roll song is first used for an advertisement it is rendered a musical eunuch.

So, to complete my brief review of *New Society* let me first of all return to the late-1980s and mention an article by John Curtice from 25 September 1987 entitled "Should Labour Turn Right?" Curtice sets out with one of many post-Election post-mortems:

"Labour enters next week's conference in a sober mood. A third crushing electoral defeat in a row, leaving it still 12 per cent adrift of the Conservatives, has resulted in demands for a radical re-evaluation of its strategy. Calls have been made both for changes in some of its central policy positions, and for the need to consider some kind of deal with the Alliance."

Well, remember the Alliance? This was all prior to the major recession of the early-1990s, which led to so many among the (new) property owning democracy losing their homes in a negative equity nightmare. I recall one of the ironic jokes of the day that focused on the 'newly wealthy' suburb of Bradley Stoke in Bristol, who were now 'sadly broke'. Curtice emphasises Thatcher's ability to manipulate a willing media in promulgating the neo-liberal propaganda of the era for a 'popular capitalism.' What he suggests in this article (as many of us argued at the time) was that Thatcher's 'revolution' was not popular in either sense of the word. But Curtice puts his finger on the inexorable shifts to the Right in the Labour Party, particularly among the leadership in one form or another.

Thus, in a Fabian tract, Islington MP Chris Smith argued that Mrs Thatcher had "convinced a substantial section of reasonably well-off working class people, in work, that they have a personal stake in capitalism'; and Tom Sawyer, chairman of the Home Policy Committee, writes of the need for Labour to appeal to "the home-owning, credit card-carrying majority (who) define their interests in a more individualistic and less collective way."

This kind of thinking led to a rapid increase in expulsions from the Party, one way to eradicate alternative voices, and opposition, to an increasingly rapid slide in to the *debacle* that became the Kinnock show in 1992. This left the way open for Blair & Co. to abduct the Labour Party and turn it in to a completely different organisation, creating among the Party faithful the kind of emotions experienced by members of the British Communist Party in 1956.

I cannot resist mentioning an article from 29 April 1988, where Adriana Caudrey discusses the "Winds of Change" in the British Social Sciences: "We are witnessing the birth of the "new social scientist". . .A new empirical streak is slowly replacing 20 or so years of Marxist rule. Apostles of the new Right predict that unless British social scientists finally shake off Marxist domination they will lag behind. Other influential figures like the Oxford social scientist, David Harvey, argue that the social sciences will lose their way if they abandon Marx."

Caudrey was, of course, guilty of merely repeating the wild generalisations about the dominance of Marxist-orientated scholarship in the social sciences. But there was a feeling that a good deal of social scientific activity was being cast in a 'folk devils' role, to which a 'moral panic' response was very predictable. Caudrey makes reference to the Economic and Social Research Council's (ESRC) document *Horizons and Opportunities*, which reported "considerable strengths and achievements of British researchers over a wide field", but at the same time "'malaise and incipient signs of decay."

Caudrey makes reference to a beleaguered ESRC, with both budget cuts and external pressures around choice of the research agenda. It is worth recalling that the Tories were keen to end any State funding of social science research, but were persuaded to 'merely' replace the Social

Science Research Council (SSRC) with the ESRC. Caudrey added that: "There has been a new-Right assault on sociologists since the early 1980s. It started when Sir Keith Joseph took the unprecedented step of ordering an investigation into the sociology department of North London Poly. His inspectors reported a Marxist bias in the syllabus and a poor standard of teaching. Since then Sociology has been considered fair game for political attack." Shades of *The History Man* here? However, it is instructive to remind ourselves, again, that this is the same Keith Joseph that talked publicly about the "cycle of deprivation" in 1972, and was instrumental in putting money from his department, the DHSS, into the joint, and long running, DHSS/SRCC project 'Studies in Deprivation and Disadvantage' (see, for example, Roger Fuller & Olive Stevenson 1983).

This article emphasises that the editorial team of *New Society* kept faith with their 1962 pledge to keep up-to-date with trends within the emerging social sciences in post-War Britain. Where these "winds of change" have taken us, both within the social sciences, and as a society, is very much bound up in the story of *New Society* itself. One aspect of the enduring value of *New Society* was that it chronicled these changes, and continuities, for better and for worse.

Finally, I must just mention that a regular column in the brief news section of the magazine was written by 'Herbivore', and the piece on 23 November 1978 is fairly typical: "My favourite children's reader is called *Shag the Otter* ('My sentiments exactly,' said a spotty youth to whom I showed the tome). At least, the book is free of sexism, which is more than can be claimed for many children's primers in which men do and women wait (in the kitchen): shimmering as they cook and hand out Elastoplast."

Raymond Williams: a biographical sketch

Since his death in January 1988, a great deal has been said and written about Raymond Williams' contribution to the intellectual and academic life of Britain. Much of this assessment has pointed to the difficulty of putting Williams into a specific category; was he a sociologist, a dramatist, a novelist, a literary critic and analyst of language, a political activist, a socialist, a Marxist? In fact at one moment or another he was all of these, and more.

Above all else Williams was a *writer* on culture and social life. He can be unequivocally regarded as the leading influence on the development of Cultural Studies in Britain. He was for many years Professor of Drama at Cambridge University.

Despite his influence on many sociologists, and on the 'cultural turn' in Sociology, there is little or no reference to Williams' writing to be found in Sociology texts. He does turn up in books, or chapters, on the mass media, but little else. Some sociologists (including this one) would argue that this says more about the narrowness of Sociology than it does about the lack of relevance in what Williams had to say, and the value of his methodology. This somewhat uneasy relationship between most Sociology and Williams (and Cultural Studies in general) will provide an interesting focus for debates in future as his influence on the analysis of British life comes to be seen as more rather than less significant.

It would not be exaggerating to say that Williams always retained a certain marginality. He was not of mainstream

English Literature or Drama or Sociology or conventional Left politics. He was on the critical margins, challenging cultural orthodoxies, in the 'border country', further accentuated by his years in Cambridge. He often commented on his not quite fitting into this heartland of the English Establishment. Being on the margins, being seen as something of a threat, is an attribute shared by many Sociologists!

Raymond Williams shared with Sociologists (and other social scientists) a concern with devising methods to more fully understand the nature of everyday life and the basis of personal and social action. He was particularly interested in the inter-relationship between the social structure of modern Britain; the nature of key social institutions, the persistence of certain roles, the continuity in patterns of power; compared and contrasted with the values and beliefs of the ordinary people.

What forms do our cultural creativity take? What are these social conditions of production? In what ways are these cultures a measure of resistance to domination, exploitation, and inequality? What can we say about the 'sites of struggle' in the day-to-day resistance of the many subjected to the continued undemocratic social control of the few?

In response to these kinds of questions it is not surprising therefore that Williams turned his attention to studies of the mass media, to literacy, and educational issues (especially adult education). He was in the forefront of debates about the commercial influences on the development of our urban and metropolitan lives, but always with an eye for the rural characteristics of the 'border country'. Williams continued to insist that a 'structure of feeling' could be conceptualised in regard to public opinion and the fashionable tendencies to everyday thought and attitudes. This depended much on the real-life material conditions of people's everyday lives *and* the sets of dominant ideologies in society at any given time. To the end of his life Williams insisted that 'culture was ordinary', that what the mass of the people created as interpretations of events, their understandings and cultural creativity was both peculiar to them in their own locality and yet indicative of more universal concerns. It was an optimistic and democratic vision of living culture and its value to the lifeblood of society.

One aspect of Raymond Williams' contribution to our lives was his fiction writing. Indeed his quite deliberate choice of fiction as a vehicle to carry and demonstrate his ideas about self and society tensions were a key to unlocking the door to understanding why we are like we are. He consistently wrote about the importance of the interface between an individual's biography, and a society's history. (And in this respect echoed the work of the American Sociologist C. Wright Mills)

In a very concrete way Williams added to our conceptual vocabulary. His continued interest in the nature (and history) of cultural forms brought him to writing *Keywords* in the 1970s. This has remained one of Williams' most widely known and popular books. (And it is worth commenting on the Penguin paperback versions of Williams' books almost certainly exposing his writing to a wider public.) Keywords are, as he put it himself, the record of an inquiry in to a vocabulary. He was endlessly intrigued by the origins and current usage of words that have continued to play a crucial part in the understandings of our everyday lives. The building blocks of our culture that say so much about the kind of society we live in now compared to both the past, and visions of the future. He was an 'archaeologist' of culture, and an 'architect' of a better, more socially just society.

All of these diverse aspects of Raymond Williams' work, *of his writing,* act as a matrix of analysis and insight, which he bestowed on us. Countless Sociologists, let alone other intellectual workers from other, complementary areas of study, owe a great debt to him. We can repay this debt in part by increasing our understanding of his contribution, and more especially by continuing to engage with our shared values, and using his approaches to influence and shape our work.

Being an agent of change: young people, democracy and cultural change

"Youth issues move up the political agenda" argued David Brindle in his *Guardian* article in 1991. His view was based largely on the Prime Minister's preparedness to listen to the case being put by the British Youth Council for a greater role in decision making by young people. A good deal of enthusiasm is attached to the idea of a ministry of youth - with cross-departmental responsibilities - much in the same way as advocated for women's concerns in the past.

The BYC has developed a 'Youth Rights Manifesto', which covers a considerable range of 'political/citizens rights', issues from Education and Training to safeguarding the environment. However, this well meaning approach does still see 'political' in a narrow, establishment politics way. Where, for example, is there any reference to young people's rights over their choice of culture activity, valued knowledge and ideas and their access to resources and amenities to be creative?

For me, these issues about rights, decision making and access, questions about authority and choices are part of long running arguments about elite cultures and the desire of small, exclusive social groups to impose their values on us all. This is especially the case for young people's lives and is an aspect of social control as far as I am concerned.

In two recent, and linked, publications, Paul Willis extends this argument on the dominance of elite cultures and the irrelevance of these 'educational' and artistic values for most people's lives. Willis is arguing for a greater acknowledgement (and funding) of what he calls *Common Culture* (Willis, 1990).

Put simply, Willis is saying that young people do have a vibrant, creative and valuable diversity of culture. They are engaged in a wide range of social processes creating and using for their own purposes, cultural and artistic products. Of course, this is related to identity shaping and expression and is certainly political in the sense that any self-conscious action to create a distinctive and semi-autonomous culture is political. Where this all becomes political is in the debates about the apportioning of value to cultures and the allocation of resources.

Willis is also extending a view that he developed about schooling in *Learning to Labour* (1978). There, he suggested that the rejection of the elitist school culture by working class 'lads' was a mini critique of the capitalist ethos. This ethos suggests that the main and valued route to high status occupation was *via* a 'good education'. Willis' 'lads' reject this for the confidence trick (dominant ideology) that it is. The 'lads' pursued their own anti-scholastic culture in their own way rendering the ideological messages redundant.

In Common Culture, Willis is once again suggesting that the overwhelming rejection (or lack of engagement with) elite, bourgeois culture by most young people is a critique of bourgeois aesthetics and values. Again, this is political, and is reminiscent of the argument that popular cultures in society are the site of struggles between contending groups. Because it is the terrain of popular cultures, including the mass media, that most people travel over in their daily lives, there are real attempts by different groups to conquer the cultural 'high ground' and profess their authority. Much of this professing is to do with which cultures should or should not be resourced, developed, opened, closed, *etc*. This is particularly significant when it comes to the allocation of public funds *via* the various agencies of the British State.

My own concept of Ideological Culture Apparatuses (ICAs) is also useful here. I have attempted to identify why and how the State and other agencies, like commercial ones, have allocated values and resources to certain cultural activities. The current Arts Council strategy debate is an interesting example of the politics of funding. The current 'debate' is supposedly engaging us citizens in decision making about the allocation of public funds. However, this activity is as minority and marginal as the use of these debated-over 'artistic' cultural products are themselves. For the lives of most (young) people the current debate about who should get 'the crumbs falling from the bourgeois culture table' is as irrelevant and exclusive as the activities themselves.

If we are going to engage in a debate about what value is placed on cultural action and production, we need to first and foremost acknowledge that the politics of this are based on conflict and not consensus criteria. In the main, cultural pursuits of young people, 'home grown' or consumed in the 'market place', are essentially of the commercial nexus. What State funding there is, continues to be a form of social, cultural and aesthetic control.

Returning to my concept of ICA, I would, of course,

acknowledge that the commercial sector produces and manipulates ideas alongside the State apparatuses (*e.g.*, education). I would certainly want to debate the positive and negative aspects (as I see it) of the ideological processes that young people are engaged in daily. The role of the media in all its guises is clearly an important area for discussion among and with the young, but not in a top-down patronising way that epitomises the 'built-in' elitism of those with power.

These necessary discussions will take place within, or in conjunction with, various agencies. For example, plenty needs to be said about the curricula currently on offer in schools and colleges across the country. It is not only HRH the Prince of Wales who would select Shakespeare ahead of other cultural products at the heart of the curriculum. The lives and works of the 'great and good' are championed in a very cross-curricula way to the exclusion or downgrading of much else. The Youth Service could do much more about the advocating of alternative perspectives on whose culture is important. The Youth Service may be better than most in giving space 'internally' to cultural diversity, but it could surely play a more vanguard role.

Access to the mass media, the most potent form of communicating in society, still remains difficult and arbitrary. More needs to be done to open up access to media resources and crucially, to 'allow' young people to be innovative, to make mistakes and learn from them, not sticking with the conventional and safe ways. There is a degree of 'youth - ghetto' media already, but we need to go well beyond this in the democratic development of resources and amenities. If we are serious about continuing to seek a lively, dynamic and healthy democracy, it is essential to develop the participatory dimension of day-to-day politics and particularly policy making.

Two recent developments in Oxfordshire seem to me examples of good practice in the battle for 'grounded aesthetics'.

First, is a proposal, still in its early stages, for a community radio. It is still to be decided whether this should be located in Oxford's College of Further Education or in a local Community or Youth Centre. The broad aim is to provide an open access medium for local (in the Country areas) people to express their views in creative and innovative ways. The primary focus will be on youth, a consistently unrepresented group locally.

The second project is already well underway. This is 'Arts work', a multi-media youth issues focused project funded by public, voluntary and private sector sponsors. Specific youth service activities have already been completed, *e.g.*, making posters as part of an environmental issues campaign. The main focus, however, is on a magazine 'MAP', the first issue of which is due out in June 1992. This is what the project coordination has to say about the magazine.

"MAP has been set up to enable young people between the ages of 14-19 to find and raise their voices. It aims to chart the terrain of young people's ideas and experiences and bring them to the attention of both young and also the wider community. In order that the magazine represents young people and their opinions, they will be involved in every aspect of its production. This will include being responsible for designing pages and images and researching and writing news and feature articles. As is in keeping with such a publication, young people that participate will ultimately take control of the magazine's editorial policy and direction."

I will be keeping a close eye on these developments, both out of general youth work interest and also because of my specific concerns about agency and change discussed in this article. I look forward to reporting on their success in the near future.

Youth Service policy making in the 1950s(1)

I was recently re-reading Ferdinand Zweig's 'The British Worker' - published in 1952.(2) It was particularly interesting to look at the chapter on the young worker given all the recent enthusiasm to offer real training for the school-leavers and potential workforce. Zweig is mainly concerned to address himself to the differences in values and attitudes towards work in particular and life in general, that he noted between young and old.

> "One general remark can be made about working-class adolescents: that nearly all of them prefer working to being at school. . .The time between 15 and 17 is a most critical age and decides the young man's whole future. The decisive point is whether he is apprenticed to a craft or supervisory grade or not. If he fails to be apprenticed, he is left, in the great majority of cases, in the labourers' or at best in the semi-skilled men's ranks for life."

If Zweig is read in conjunction with say Sillitoe's *Saturday Night and Sunday Morning* (1958) or the Crowther Report: 15-18 (1959), a fascinating picture of the young worker - potential and actual, begins to appear. Of course, most of this, like other writing of the time, is actually about the young working class male; certainly this is so if we are looking at connections with the Youth Service.

"Arthur walked into a huge corridor, searching an inside pocket for his clocking-in card and noticing, as on every morning since he was fifteen - except for a two-year break in the Army - the factory smell of oil-suds, machinery, and shaved steel that surrounded you with an air in which pimples grew and prospered on your face and shoulders, that would have turned you into one big pimple if you did not spend half an hour over the scullery sink every night getting rid of the biggest bastards. What a life, he thought. Hard work and good wages and a smell all day that turns your guts." [3]

- *Saturday Night and Sunday Morning* (1958), Alan Sillitoe

". . .Our terms of reference require us to consider changing social needs. In every aspect of education and at every stage of our thinking we have been keenly aware of the way in which social conditions, attitudes and habits affect what education can achieve . . . two main directions of change …seem especially important for their impact on teenagers and for the way in which they define some of the objectives of educational policy. The first is the emancipation, or isolation, of the individual (it can be looked at

both ways) and the rejection of traditional
authority, the second, the conquest of the field
of communications by the mass production
techniques which were first applied to the
manufacture of goods." [4]

- Crowther Report (1959)

My aim in this article is to discuss the formation of Youth
Service policy in the 1950s. I am concerned to look at the
processes that lead to the formulation of this or that policy
and the forces that came to bear on that formulation.
Whether all of these competing and complementary forces
were realised in the eventual policies for the Youth Service is
another matter, of course, and I am very anxious to explore
the alternative lines of development in those years. Under-
standably perhaps a good deal of this article will be
concerned with the Youth Service policy paradigm of the
1950s, but I want to set that in context.

To spread out my period of interest, it is necessary to
have to look at policy discussion and formulation, the actual
function of the 'Youth Service', the nature of youth - in all its
heterogeneity, from at least 1939. It is commonplace to
acknowledge the impact of War on public and social
administration, and this is certainly the case with the Youth
Service. Consideration of the War and immediate post-War
period, adds a considerable amount to my brief analysis of
Youth Service policy making in the 1950s. I am also very
conscious of the Albermarle Report [5] hanging over me as I
write about the 1950s.

One of the most important issues in the formation of the

Youth Service after the War was the nature of relationships between the agencies of the State - the statutory sector, and the agencies of the voluntary sector. Up until 1939, the voluntary sector was the major influence in 'youth' organisation. One of the factors that affect the eventual outcome is the role of the voluntary agencies. This article addresses the 'partnership', the post-War settlement, the co-existence and consensus that it was argued would form the impetus and basis for the Youth Service. One of the issues of the 1950s is whether or not this partnership was a viable proposition. Did the partnership survive the ups and downs of policy making in the light of changed and changing circumstances, attitudes and so on? The answer in brief is yes and no: it was a viable proposition, but it did not survive.

A good deal of this article is devoted to an analysis of Albermarle, particularly the critical posture that the Report took in its analysis of the post-War Youth Service and the needs for the future. However, it is an all too easy trap to fall into to start with Albermarle as if what preceded that report would, of historical necessity, lead to their account in 1960. These persons, as 'individuals' and/or members of organisations and institutions, who were inextricably tied-up in the formulation of Youth Service policy between 1939 and 1959 did not do what they did in anticipation of the Albermarle Report in 1960.

Some, with the benefit of hindsight, argue that Albermarle was nemesis, but that argument overlooks one or two interesting sub-plots.

What does concern me is the way in which Youth Service

policy making has been inconsistent. One factor that I have already alluded to, and must develop here, is the manner in which the development of post-War youth, as a reality and as an ideological construct, has some bearing on the formulation of policies for 'youth in general' in areas such as education, delinquency, family and personal sexual relations, and the formulation of policies for the Youth Service in particular. These relations between actuality, ideology and policy making are complex to say the least, even given the usual difficulties that exist in sorting out fact from fiction.

I started out by suggesting that a novel (in this case *Saturday Night and Sunday Morning*) might prove useful in helping to put together an understanding of post-War youth - particularly in relation to work and leisure. I should add before proceeding with any analysis of 'youth' in the 1950s that problems do exist about the telling and retelling of what it was like to be young. Moreover, we know more than enough about the changes in Youth Service policy in relation to other youth-orientated policies in recent years to underline the point that what needs to be done about youth is a moveable feast at the best of times. Given radical changes in government, as was the case in 1979, matters can at times take a more decisive lurch in one direction or another.

At certain moments in the history of the Youth Service and this is certainly true of the 1939-45 period, an ideal position is formulated by the policy makers, matters of principle are stated, only to be retreated from fairly quickly. It is interesting to assess all factors that brought the War-time State to create a set of policies and encourage a range of institutional developments and then more or less drop them.

It is also important to emphasise that the 'creation' of the Youth Service in the War years set the seal on many years of work by many professionals working in this field of social service. It also, importantly, legitimated a whole new era of professional development, which in turn has been affected by the ups and downs in the Youth Service.

Between 1939 and the issue of the Board of Education circular 1486, 'In the Service of Youth', and 1960, with the publication of the Albermarle Report on the Youth Service in England and Wales, the orientation of the Youth Service appears to change. In 1939 there was an attempt to move away from earlier but relevant concerns with physical fitness to one of integrating the young (officially, 15-20 years) into society. This project attempted to give the young a more adult role to play in the community, especially in the 'post-War' reconstruction of society and social life.

Essentially related to this was the drive to integrate and coordinate the various strands of provision for the young already in existence.

It appears that the policy makers were appreciative of the effort made by the numerous voluntary bodies, but were anxious to see this consolidated and broadened *via* funding and centralisation by the State.

By the end of the 1950s, this project had apparently gone sour. The Youth Service was, ideologically, in disarray. Why did this happen? What forces were at work between 1939, and the late fifties that influenced, even dictated the change in State Policy? How did youth and society change in that fifteen year post-War period that led Albermarle to initiate the change of policy and set into motion the so-called 'bricks and mortar' phase of the Youth Service? Did this change represent a contraction in the aims of the State, of the policy makers?

It may well be that the condition of youth was such that the State did not feel it essential to provide a service of any kind, but especially one that underwrote the integrative role of the agents of socialisation and social control in society. Perhaps there was a general belief that youth would represent a threat to order, or become a distinctive social problem and that little or nothing had to be done about the special provisions demanded in a later phase by Albermarle?

Did Albermarle mark recognition of the separateness of youth, socially and culturally and bring to a close the period when a belief existed in society that youth could be successfully incorporated and integrated into the normative order of proper adult society? It is certainly possible to perceive the development of a discourse that increasingly marginalises youth culturally and ideologically, the association of youth with the creation and reproduction of deviant categories.

It is also necessary to stress the influence of the general post-1944 developments in 'Welfare' provision. It is necessary to do this because if I am to attempt to assess the magnitude of social and cultural change that has affected youth and Youth Service policy, the affects of the welfare provision on post-War British society is clearly a substantial factor and germane to my discussion. Not the least of my concerns here is the role of the expenditure controls in the Youth Service.

Whatever sums of money were envisaged in 1939 to set

up and run the Youth Service, were either not sufficient, or were quite drastically cut back during the following years. No matter how admirable and necessary the Service may have been in the eyes of successive governments, they were not prepared to make a financial commitment even in line with the fairly modest targets of War years. It is certainly true that Albermarle saw this shortfall of funds as a major factor in the failings of the Youth Service. While this appears to be true, a reductionist approach must be avoided here at the expense of a more culturally complex argument.

Before looking at the 1950s in much more detail, it is useful to look forward to Albermarle and back to the 1939-1945 War. Initially, to place Albermarle's project in a context, the report begins with the 'conventional wisdom' criteria for the Committee's work.

> "We were appointed at a most crucial time. First, because several aspects of national life, to which the Youth Service is particularly relevant, are today causing widespread and acute concern. These include serious short-term problems, such as that of the 'bulge' in the adolescent population. They include also much more complex and continuous elements of social change, elements to which adolescents are responding sharply and often in ways which adults find puzzling or shocking. Second, because it soon became clear to us that the Youth Service itself is in a critical condition." [6]

What emerges from Albermarle is that many people within the political policy making and professional bureaucratic elites had dedicated themselves to the development of a comprehensively more effective, national Youth Service. They were disappointed at the failure to achieve this ideal. Whether they were naive to believe that the relatively adventurous goals set in the 1939-1945 period could be achieved is another matter. It is not uncommon for groups of well-informed and sincerely motivated professionals to pursue goals in their chosen field with a certainty of their appropriateness and successful achievement, which is not matched by the policy makers in general. One of the features of the period between 1945 and 1960 is the way in which the aims of the Youth Service devotees were gradually eroded, so that by 1960 there is almost the sense of having to start the project over again. As Jeffs has pointed out, the setbacks were perhaps too numerous to sustain the 'project' in any unified form at all, and this may have been particularly true of cuts in funding after 1945. [7]

Sir John Maud was Permanent Secretary to the Ministry of Education in 1951 and he spoke on two related aspects of the Youth Service in that year. Firstly he warned 'the Youth Service' that those concerned with it could only expect a reduction in their already dwindling resources and a reducing share of education expenditure in the future. He also spoke of the 'raw deal' that the Youth Service had had. In this, as in other contemporary assessments of the Youth Service's relative decline, there is almost a sense of betrayal.

"In 1951 the King George's Jubilee Trust

called a two-day conference at Ashbridge to debate the 'Youth Service of Tomorrow'. By then it was apparent that the expansion that had seemed a real possibility in the early and mid 1940s was not going to take place. . .The report of the conference makes somewhat sombre reading: it talks of declining membership and seemingly intractable problems 'of not enough money, not enough buildings, and too few people as leaders', as policy of fewer organisations and fewer organisers and administrators." [8]

This conference, which brought together representatives from voluntary organisations and local authorities, was an explicit attempt to influence prevailing Government attitudes and policymaking. The State had been instrumental in bringing the two wings of the 'Youth Service' together and, so it seemed, let them down together. This was clearly a post-1945 judgement by Government, as all the indicators in 1939 and even in 1944, were that the 'marriage' of the voluntary and the statutory sectors would actually improve the conditions and future prospects of the 'Youth Service'.

In many ways those people from the voluntary sector could feel justified in feeling lulled into a false sense of security and being 'mugged' along the way. However, the 'mugger' was clearly 'the State', or more precisely 'Governments of the day', as those within the Local Authorities who had been drawn into partnership with the voluntary agencies were equally as dedicated to the Service and as equally dismayed, upset and disappointed by the changes in attitude and policy.

This relationship of the two sectors of the Service is certainly important in terms of the period after Albermarle, where gradually the dominance and influence of the voluntary sector is reduced in favour of the role of Local Authorities. But up to 1939 and certainly between 1939 and 1960, the voluntary sector remained the 'senior' partner.

Before 1945 the voluntary service was, to all intents and purposes, the Youth Service. The gradual development of a statutory Service during the War years made little significant change and, indeed, in the years that followed the War the relationship between the two remained an ambiguous one. Despite their evident difficulties there was a sense that the Youth Service was here to stay. Authorities and voluntary bodies responded vigorously, in spite of early difficulties of adjustment, a creditable measure of cooperation was achieved. The Service was written about and youth workers of the time spoke of the interest and enthusiasm of the public. Universities and university colleges offered training courses for professional leaders and as the War ended the Service seemed full of promise.

However, as Eggleston points out, the seeds of the takeover were evidently sown in this War-time phase of establishing the partnership and encouraging cross-fertilisation of sectors, through the application of a fairly common ideology.

> "Through the fifties the development of the statutory service continued, often in

association with a parallel development of
further education facilities. Though, as with
all other educational development, progress
varied with the prevailing economic
conditions. Nonetheless, the statutory service
was still considered in many areas to serve a
gap-filling role: certainly it was not in any
sense in competition with the established
voluntary organisations, though the very
existence of an alternative set of provisions
had an unquestionable effect on the voluntary
bodies." [9]

The Albermarle report reflects this development of
partnership and also underlines the feeling of optimism that
prevailed in the new Youth Service constituency despite the
obvious problems that were in existence.

"In 1939 the Board of Education called the
Youth Service into being with the issue of a
single circular. This could not have happened
but for what had gone before. . .What the
Board did at the start of the War was to bring.
. .three parties, State, education authority and
voluntary organisation, into a working
arrangement to which the term 'Youth
Service' has ever since been given".

In Circular 1486 the Board undertook "a
direct responsibility for youth welfare". The

President had set up a National Youth
Committee and local education authorities
were called on to set up youth committees of
their own. Key phrases in the circular were:
"close association of local education
authorities and voluntary bodies in full
partnership in a common enterprise" . . .
"ordered scheme of local provision". .
"indicate the lines on which a real advance
can be made under more favourable
conditions". . . "new constructive outlets".
Later circulars made it clear that the Board
regarded the Youth Service as a permanent
part of education. So did the White Paper on
Education Reconstruction (1943), which gave
a separate section to the Youth Service. The
McNair Report (1944) encouraged the public
to think of youth leadership as a profession,
which ought to have proper conditions of
training and service. The Youth Advisory
Council (the successor to the National Youth
Committee) produced two reports (1943 and
1945), which were full of hope for the future
of the Service. Finally the Education Act,
1944, not only made it a duty on authorities to
do what they were already doing out of
goodwill, but offered in addition, the county
college, a mighty ally to the Youth Service.

In 1945, the Ministry of Education made it
plain that they did not intend for the present

to put into effect the McNair recommendations about youth leaders. All the same the outlook still seemed bright enough to attract numbers of able men and women leaving the armed forces into the courses for professional leaders offered by universities and voluntary organisations. For two or three years longer the Service made some progress. It continued to be widely discussed and four of the Ministry's pamphlets published between 1945 and 1949 took it into serious account. Then the wind began to blow cold. With one economic crisis after another the Ministry could do no more than indicate that the Youth Service (with other forms of "learning for leisure") must be held back to allow, first, for the drive for new school places and later for the development of technical education. The county college looked as far off as ever. The Jackson Committee (1949) and the Fletcher Committee (1951) produced reports on the training and conditions of service of professional youth leaders. Neither was put into effect. The flow of recruits shrank, the number of full-time leaders fell away and the university and other full-time courses closed down one by one until today only three survive. With the Ministry unable to give the signal for advance certain authorities lost heart. Public interest

flagged too, and not surprisingly voluntary
bodies felt the effect. It is easy to over-expose
the picture and to fail to do justice to the good
and valiant work, which has been done since
the War and is still being done. All the same
the Youth Service has not been given the
treatment it hoped for and thought it
deserved and has suffered in morale and
public esteem in consequence". [10]

It is important to recognise the ideological argument
bound up in this statement by Albermarle. It retains the
notion of the 'post-War', especially 1944, concern with the
achievement of political consensus.

The 'reality' of embourgeoisement, convergence, and
relative affluence came later and cannot be easily reduced in
cause and effect to the achievement of consensus. What is
particularly significant about the 1944 Education Act is that it
provided the institutionalised framework and context for the
continuing discourse about schooling, and life after school, to
the exclusion of other strategies. [11]

The particular relevance of this for the Youth Service was
that the opportunity was created for a new liaison between
State and voluntary provision and that the *need* for a service
to enhance the emerging obsessions with 'character building'
and 'citizenship' was legitimated by the State's legislative
intervention. The 'universatising' character and intention of
educational legislation gave an impetus for the job of
citizenship building to be carried on and developed beyond
the limits of the school. Where the project eventually failed

was that despite the encouraging words from the Board and Ministry of Education and in the 1944 Act, the Governments of the fifties were not at all sure that the *reinforcement* role of the Youth Service was really necessary.

I would argue that it is important to consider the influence of existing institutional values, structures and practices of the long established youth clubs and organisations in influencing or determining policy making. Equally as important in its own way is to recognise the influence of the range of quasi-scientific notions of adolescence in both the 1944 Act and the emergence of the Youth Service.

Board of Education circular 1516 (ref. 27.6.40) [12] set the tone for the new Youth Service in emphasising the character-building role of the Service in tandem with the drive for citizenship *within* the free liberal association framework of the new pluralist society. It was implicit that this was training for the necessary adult role acceptance to maintain the normative order. What is more explicit in the official literature of the 1940s is the concern with the 'indirect' nature of this socialisation. Yes, of course Youth Service workers were agents of socialisation and social control, but their role was not seen to be a coercive one. Indeed, the widely held assumption was that a coercive role would not be needed, as young people would naturally gravitate to the Service that provided them with the dual opportunity to sit at the feet of their elders and share with their peers the various recreational activities that would bring pleasure and a greater understanding of their part in society.

Wolfenden was the first chairman of the Youth Advisory

Council, appointed by the President of the Board of Education in 1942, to advise on matters relating to the Youth Service. Wolfenden is linked with two crucial documents establishing the tone of the service. These two reports, ('The Youth Service after the War' 1943 and 'The Purpose and Content of the Youth Service' 1945-HMSO), [13] discussed the need for a Service, the role of youth in the War, the nature of the 'curriculum' to be offered, even the kind of leadership required. These Reports have a tone that reflects the influence of public school and grammar school values.

Indeed, Wolfenden was the Headmaster of Uppingham School in 1943 and of Shrewsbury School by 1945. The 1943 Report placed great store on the courage of the young in the War and looking beyond the end of hostilities anticipated the continued fortitude of the younger generation.

> "We are convinced that they will respond to the challenge of the post-War world just as courageously as they have met the challenge of War, if only they can be offered as careful and thorough a training for citizenship as they are now given for battle. Given such training, we believe that the great majority of them will grow up to be individuals physically, mentally and spiritually capable of playing their full part as adult members of the kind of society we wish to see, that is, a society which can only function effectively if all its members take an informed and responsible share in its activities". [14]

One interesting aspect of this 'training and citizenship' business is the development, both welcomed and alarming, of armed forces education, which we know enough about to see what a significant influence it had on the 1945 General Election and beyond. [15]

The 1943 report anticipated a post-War plurality that must have scared many sections of the British elite. Many of those in custody of the great British heritage of privilege and inequality could not have begun to contemplate this awful prospect.

> "We neither expect nor wish all young people
> to grow up holding the same views, for if they
> did both they and the body politic would be
> the poorer. We want each one of them to
> come to see that the fullest life, both for
> himself and for his community, demands that
> he should recognise duties and
> responsibilities as well as enjoy rights and
> benefits. We want to see them all grounded
> in the principal loyalties of a sound
> civilisation, their loyalty to God, the King and
> Country, to their family, to their neighbour
> and to their unit of livelihood. We believe
> that bringing up young people to practise
> these loyalties will give disciplined freedom
> to society and yield what is due to both the
> individual and the community". [16]

This path of development for the formation of young persons' values, attitudes and behaviour is complemented by the functions of the Youth Service itself. Of some interest here is the clearly expressed view that some young persons would be developed and guided by their schooling and career aims, their inheritance or cultural capital. The perceived model of upper and middle class education as an agency of socialisation and social control is that it reproduced the inclusive nature of things. However, the situation is different for the non-academic, and by definition, working class young person, who is still faced with schooling as an agency of social control. This report warns against the problems induced by in 'over academic' development of the schooling and youth services.

> "The majority of young people do not find
> satisfaction in an academic atmosphere even
> during school years... to confront them again
> in the Youth Service with the same academic
> and intellectual standards in which they could
> find no significance at school will drive them
> out of any form of youth organisation
> forever". [17]

The Youth Service had its foundations built on 'shifting sand', and had fallen back on its traditional mixture of *ad hocism* and philanthropy. The organisers and associates of the Service after 1945 looked to the Ministry of Education for a lead, and for an ally in the competition and bidding for resources. This was to be a major error of judgement.

Albermarle pointed to good work done, local enthusiasm and high hopes, despite the lack of support from the State.

How then, other than for purely financial reasons, can we explain the change of heart by post-War government? What I would argue is that Albermarle and the reports and discourse after 1960 indicate that a major error of judgement was made by the State.

It might well be that the State policy makers relied on an inadequate, indeed out of date, analysis of the nature of youth and society. I would want to suggest the following as part of what the government's assessment of youth seemed to omit or overlook or choose to ignore and put the discussion on policy making made above into a wider context.

A large body of sociological writing since the 1950s has emphasised one of the most significant changes in the life of the industrial population: the movement from work to leisure. This movement has not only been in terms of hours per week devoted to work or non-work activities, but to a re-orientation in the advanced industrial societies towards the prime pursuit of leisure, enjoyment and recreation. The 'leisure consumers' have become vitally important to the creation of wealth in industrial society. Again this development is part of wider, even more far reaching changes. First, it is evident in the movement away from industrial societies dominated by manufacturing production to ones greatly influenced, if not yet dominated by service industry; and, second, in the major movement away from concentration on the problems of production to those of consumption. This series of fundamental changes are usually referred to as post-industrialism and post-scarcity. The latter concept celebrates the point of development in industrial society when the advances in technology related to altered production organisation has provided the opportunity for vast numbers of people to be released from time in the workplace. Larkin[18] makes great play with the fact of a significant shift from cultural emphasis on 'work time' to cultural emphasis on leisure; but, even he fails to underline the fact that the societal development of leisure was also, essentially, an economic development. The expansion in the leisure 'industries', most, but not all, in the service sector, has been one of the most significant areas of corporately managed economic expansion since the 1950s. Indeed, I would argue that this development is a further episode in social reproduction in the advanced industrial societies. Clearly the very living out of leisure, the consumption that takes place in this time and, largely, the values associated with its prosecution are ways in which the forces and relations of production in society are reproduced and maintained. [19]

There is an 'illusion' of freedom in the cultural ambiance of leisure that is a marked aspect of its ideological character. However, as Larkin also suggests, post-War youth are essentially part of the process whereby desires have replaced needs. This cultural change is part of, not separate from, the development of post-industrial, post-scarcity society where 'youth' as a social formation has been created. Youth, as a *socially* constructed formation arrived simultaneously, indeed largely as a consequence of, these other social and economic changes.

The official reports dealing with the emergence and development of a Youth Service in the UK reflect the contradictions and confusions that arise from these changes. The various reports, up to and including Albermarle, concentrate on the functional necessity of adequate socialisation on the one hand, while also recognising the disequilibria caused by 'adolescence' on the other. However, the concern with personal physiological and psychological development neglects the changed 'world' in which young people are 'growing up'.

It is not my intention to enter into a lengthy account of the emergence of post-War 'youth', but what is certainly significant is that the policy makers either did not understand the nature of the arrival of 'youth', or indeed *did* have an inkling of what was happening and chose not to communicate their thoughts publicly. Certainly by the time of Albermarle, the policy makers in the field of the Youth Service did realise that most of the post-War project had gone dreadfully wrong, the Youth Service was, according to Albermarle, moribund, unresponsive and dying on its feet.

Albermarle tried to set the Youth Service on a new course, away from an agency of socialisation that focused attention upon the inculcation of traditional bourgeois values (loyalty to God, King and Country, family, neighbour, employer and private property), to a Service that not only recognised the plurality of the post-War social structure, and the uniqueness of 'youth', but also sought to both retreat behind youth club doors, entertaining the young into conformity while offering what specialist assistance and advice the young were prepared to seek or take.

Fyvel is typical of many critics of post-War youth writing at the time of Albermarle.[20] One of the central features of Fyvel's analysis was the shock he registered on behalf of many adults that an increasing number of young people were deviant despite all that was on offer in the post-1950 welfare state world. Fyvel wrote a reassessment of his book in 1978, which offers an interesting insight into his more explicit thesis.

> "What I saw as finally crumbling by the
> fifties was the classical bourgeois capitalist
> society dominated by the urban middle class.
> This society consolidated its status in the 19th
> century and was based on exclusive upper
> middle class economic privilege, buttressed
> by domestic servants. It was filled with
> institutions and patriarchal figures
> embodying moral authority.
> By the 'fifties, this society was being rapidly
> replaced by the British consumer society.
> So, but more slowly, was its system of moral
> authority; deference to upper class and state
> authority; to employers, the law, the police,
> the churches and teachers and to parents in
> the family which had held society together. A
> new authority was assumed by the
> advertisers, entertainers and other hedonistic
> voices of the consumer society". [21]

I would therefore re-emphasise the disjuncture that exists

between the social and cultural forces that comprise the framework of the Youth Service. The role of Government has been interventionist but changeable. The partnership of statutory local authority and voluntary agencies has always been an uncertain, localised and ambiguous affair. Some LEAs have done much to cement the post-War foundations, others, as Albermarle pointed out, took fright or became greedy for influence and set off in their own direction. Collectively, these agencies have tended to dictate the aims and objectives of the Youth Service and assumed or hoped that it would attract the usage of the young. As I have argued above, the various agencies overlooked too much to be remotely successful and when faced with the recalcitrance or pusillanimous-ness of youth, fell back on traditional irrational authoritarianism to resolve their problems. The socialisation process of society assumes enormous contradictions in those conditions. [22]

It is now appropriate to expand my assessment of the 1950s developments in the Youth Service, set against the paradigm of Youth in that period and what actually seems was happening then.

I have already cited the Crowther Report and it is worth devoting more time to it. There is an element of the mass culture debate running through this Report. The liberality of the new age is clearly a cause for rejoicing and concern. It is all very well to open up new frontiers for the young, but the consequent changes may not always be those desired by the Establishment. "Emancipation and the moral code" therefore features as a destructive issue and concern in Crowther. There are, for example, changes in the nature of the family.

What Fletcher [23] and other sociologists of the 1950s were to call the democratisation of the family, is seen by Crowther as a mixed blessing. Older teenagers "are no longer beholden to their parents for their pleasures". [24] Levels of expectations amongst the young have changed, as have staying in and going out patterns. The Report points to a break up of the traditional moral order, which in turn, of course, affects the family and its significance as an agent of socialisation and social control. Needless to say, the thorny issue of sexual ethics is raised and significantly enough is run into a substantial consideration of juvenile delinquency. Mays [25] and even worse, Burt, [26] are taken as markers for an analysis of the factors leading to a steady increase in delinquency. Mays is quoted, for example, as underlining one central problem of the 1950s for the Establishment, that the young are not only deviant, they are also defiant! A good many issues are rolled up together here, for example, the pressure on the traditional community, the effects of the War on children, the lack of relevance in schooling for older children. The Crowther Report argues that in the past a man stuck loyally to the tradition, custom and practice of his father and only changed in dire circumstances, but in the 1950s, people are giving up their old loyalties. This is certainly true of the young, and once again the unfortunate influences of the media are cited.

It is interesting here to reflect upon the mass culture debate in conjunction with delinquency and the like. Fyvel always argued that the liberal establishment were shocked by the disagreeable and ungrateful nature of the young in the 1950s. Despite all the wonders of the welfare state, the young, or significant sections of it anyway, remained disaffected and recalcitrant. The glitter of the emergent pop culture, in its wider sense, upset the establishment (in schools and elsewhere) and they were right to suspect that they were fighting a losing battle. They were, of course, not prepared to fight the entrepreneurs of the new world media head on, instead they preferred to attempt to dilute the product, or distract the potential audience/activists. They failed.

The American experience of this problem came earlier and was different in the sense that the salesmanship, consumption, acquisitiveness and status -obsessed culture was instrumental in the formation of the media. Randall Jarrell was able to write in the early 1960s with absolute certainty that: ". . .inside every fat man there is a man who is starving, part of you is being starved to death and the rest of you is being stuffed to death". [27] Crowther put it much more in terms of the passage of a golden era of adult authority:

> ". . .all that has happened is the substitution of the
> public opinion of their peers for the wisdom of the
> pages. Teenage opinion is often badly informed, fickle
> and superficial. How should it be otherwise? Of all age-
> groups, the teenagers are most exposed to the impact of
> the 'mass media' of communication".[28]

Crowther asserts that the confluence of new demands, pressures, situations and tastes, places an extra burden of responsibility on the local authority to provide support for the young.

"The teenagers with whom we are concerned
need, perhaps before all else, to find a faith to
live by. They will not all find precisely the
same faith and some will not find any.
Education can and should play some part in
their search. It can assure them that there is
something to search for and it can show them
where to look and what other men have
found". [29]

Crowther rests its case in this segment of its influence by
arguing that society ought not to withdraw from the young
worker the help it gave to the school student.

The late 1950s and early 1960s was an interesting period
of reforming legislation particularly in relation to what Stuart
Hall and others have called, the legislation of consent.[30] The
Home Secretaryships of Butler and Jenkins were marked by
an attempt to direct growing public concerns about personal
and inter-personal liberality into parliamentary action. The
theme of moral panics is clearly to be identified in this
period, with periods of panic reasonably well related to
significant issues and events of the hour.   Certainly the
mobilisation of bias is a significant issue in these years and
besides anything else that might be considered it is fruitful to
look at what was being argued for and against youth and the
Youth Service within the politics of reform. The importance
of residual and emergent values cannot be over-estimated
here, in piecing together a picture of the case being put for
and against the development of the Youth Service.

It would   seem,   for   example,   that   the   increasingly interventionist 'state' of the 1950s deliberately chose to bifurcate youth issues, by setting the normal sharply apart from the abnormal. There was the tendency then to deal with youth in a way that reinforced the idea that the troublemakers, the disaffected and so on, could and should, be regarded as a special category of young persons. Delinquency, for example, increasingly becomes a 'way of life' for a minority from the State's perspective of young persons and not a 'fact of life' for the majority. The Interventionist State's 'policy', administrative strategy of isolation, ghetto-ization of social problems as a practical means of dealing with youth issues is increasingly marked.

In conclusion, let me attempt to draw together some of the threads of my arguments on the emergence of a State sanctioned, if not always State financed and run Youth Service. Throughout this article I have stressed the War-time and immediate post-War context of public and social administration in relation to the development of ideas about what form efforts for creating a Youth Service could and should take. Hopefully, I have emphasised the mixture of hopeful openness and continued desire for social control processes in the collective minds of the administrators, *etc.*, of the time. The reconstruction of Britain, in so many senses that do not need elaborating here, certainly includes major discussion throughout society about the nature of economic and social relations and the desired nature of social change to bring about the 'new and good society'.

The social democratic/pluralist faith in the evolutionary democratisation of society is a central focus of debate here, particularly with regard to the working class. What part were 'they' to play, be allowed to play, *etc.,* in the shaping of post-War society? Changes to and within the working class are, by definition, part of the material for discussion. It may well have been the case that those persons and classes with power to shape the future of society assumed that the working class share of power or life chances or whatever, would remain much the same; they would just have a more comfortable life perhaps? Less of their children would go hungry and die young? More of their young would go a little beyond the four Rs? More young adults would obtain and retain a job, pay their national insurance, have a not too overcrowded and damp-free place to live? As we all know, the place where the vision of the 'Brave New World' for all and the Consumer(ised) Society meet, was, have become, an unholy mess.

The post-War generation of young persons and those engaged in the development of young persons and Youth Services were, whether they were self-conscious of it or not, right in the thick of this. The cultural/political struggles that took place; or even, of course, crucially perhaps, did not take place, at the end of the War, left their indelible mark on the Youth Service that emerged.

The debate about the fate of the Working Class and the Working Class Community in the light of all these desired and imposed, struggled for and reluctantly conceded, changes, has been a considerable one.[31] The analysis of Youth Service policy making should be seen as contributing to and learning from, this broader debate.

NOTES:

1. This article first appeared in *Youth and Policy* No. 19, 1987.

2. ZWEIG, F. *The British Worker*. Penguin, 1952.

3. SILLITOE, A. *Saturday Night and Sunday Morning*. Pan, 1958.

4. CROWTHER REPORT. (15 to 18) Min. of Ed. HMSO, 1959 *p.36*.

5. ALBERMARLE. Min. of Ed. *The Youth Service in England and Wales*. HMSO, 1960.

6. *Ibid*.

7. JEFFS, A. J. *Young People and The Youth Service*. RKP, 1979.

8. *Ibid p.29*.

9. EGGLESTON, J. *Adolescence and Community. The Youth Service in Britain*. Arnold, 1976, *p.16*.

10. Albermarle *op. cit.*

11. BARON, S. *et. al. Unpopular Education. Schooling and Social Democracy in England, 1944-1981*. Hutchinson, 1981.

12. Board of Education Circular 1516. HMSO, 1940.

13. Board of Education. *The Youth Service after the War*. (The first). Report of the Youth Advisory Council. HMSO, 1943. Ministry of Education. *The purpose and Content of the Youth Service*. (The second) Report of the Y.A.C. HMSO, 1945. J. WOLFENDON was chairman for both Reports.

14. *Ibid p.5/6*.

15. GRANT, N. *Citizen Soldiers: Army Education in World War 2. in Formations of Nation and People*. Ed. by Bennett, T. *et al* RKP, 1984.

16 Board of Education. 1943. *Op cit* p.6.

17. *Ibid p.10*.

18. LARKIN, R.W. *Suburban Youth in Cultural Crisis*. OUP, 1979.

19. CLARK, J. and CRITCHER, C. *The Devil Makes Work. Leisure in Capitalist Britain*. MacMillan, 1985.

20. FYVEL, T.R. *The Insecure Offenders: Rebellious Youth in the Welfare State*. Penguin, 1961.

21. FYVEL, T.R. *The 'Insecure Offenders' in retrospect*. New Society, (20.7.78, p.128.)

22. See ASTLEY, J. *Industrial-Urban Culture, Youth and the Problem of*

Socialisation. in The Social Science Teacher, Vol.8, No.2, 1978.

23. FLETCHER, R. *Family and Marriage in Britain*. Penguin, 1962.

24. Crowther Report. *op cit* p.36.

25. MAYS, J. *The Young Pretenders*. Sphere, 1969.

26. BURT, C. *The Young Delinquent*. ULP, 1969.

27. JARRELL, R. *A Sad Heart at the Supermarket*. Farrar, Straus & Giroux, 1962.

28. Crowther Report. *op cit* p.43.

29. *Ibid* p.44.

30. HALL, S. *Reformism and the Legislation of Consent in Permissiveness and Control*: *the fate of the Sixties Legislation*. *Edited by* J. Clark *et al*. MacMillan, 1980.

31. See for example: Clark, J. *et al*. *Working Class Culture. Studies in history and theory*. Hutchinson, 1979. George, V. and Wilding, P. *Ideology and Social Welfare*. RKP, 1976. Hoggart, R. *The Uses of Literacy*. Penguin, 1958. Rojeck, C. *Capitalism and Leisure Theory*. Tavistock, 1985. Seabrook, J. *What went wrong?* Gollancz, 1978. *A World Still to Win. The Reconstruction of the Post-War Working Class* (with Trevor Blackwell) faber & faber, 1985.

Professions, Professionals, and Power

THE GROWTH OF PROFESSIONS

Although professional workers existed before the early nineteenth century, it was the rapid process of industrialisation, with rationalisation, specialisation of production and intensified division of labour that created the situation where so-called professional workers have become an integral part of society. There are some well-known attempts to rationalise the growth of professions. Are there common characteristics that could help to qualify or disqualify occupational groups? Millerson (64) in his study, developed six traits of the 'model' profession:

- A skill based on theoretical knowledge
- An extensive period of education
- The testing of competence before admission to the profession
- The existence of a code of conduct
- A theme of public service
- The freedom of the profession to regulate itself.

Professionalisation has been complementary to the process whereby occupation has become the typical basis of differentiation in society. Jencks in the USA and Boudon in France, have been typical of sociologists who have stressed the rise of the 'meritocratic' society, where educational success is increasingly valued as the means of achieving the end of access to such high status occupations as the

professions. Many occupational groups aspiring to professional status have sought to use educational achievement as
the lever to elevate them to a higher rung in the occupational hierarchy. This process of professionalisation has
been further accelerated by an increasingly democratic
society. It is interesting and often paradoxical that the late
19th and 20th century demands for social reforms, which
have created extensive welfare provision and a public
service sector, brought about the conditions for the rapid
growth of professional occupations. The increase in the size
of the professions and the number of professional
occupations was augmented by other changes in post-War
British society, such as the reforms in secondary education.
These reforms gave a limited access to professional work to
people otherwise excluded by lack of acceptable social
background, and/or education. Many of the boys and girls of
the upper working class, were able to move in socially
mobile ways into occupations, rewards, conditions and
status that their parents could not have enjoyed (Jackson &
Marsden, 1962).

Movement took place into 'white-collar', and often public
sector jobs. However, it might be argued that a good deal of
this movement was intra, rather than inter, class.

Service industries especially have expanded in the last
thirty years in Britain or elsewhere. The State's intervention
into the Economy, and increasingly into the everyday lives
of citizens, has meant the creation of jobs that have, in turn,
been filled by aspiring professionals, newly educationally
accredited, to fill such occupational roles.

PROFESSIONALISATION AND SOCIAL MOBILITY

Education and paper qualifications have increasingly become the arbiter of someone's fitness for access to a professional occupation (Young, 58, Jackson & Marsden, 1962). However, it would be injudicious to over-estimate the degree of even upper-working class access to the professions. Goldthorpe's study (1979) emphasises the limited nature of access to what he calls the 'service-class' - people with well-paid jobs with career prospects in the professions. The 1979 Nuffield surveys indicate that men born between 1908 and 1917 and brought up between the wars in working-class families had a 14 per cent % chance of reaching the 'service-class'.

For men born to similar families between 1938 and 1947, the chance had risen to 18 per cent. However, the study also shows that those men born into such professional families in the 1938-47 period had an even greater prospect of achieving access to a professional occupation than the 1908-17 generation. This study would seem to suggest that ascribed status is still a distinctive feature of post-war Britain.

PROFESSIONS AND ELITES

One important feature of professionalisation in the last hundred years has been the extent to which this occupational group, wide as it is, has come to be dominant as advisers to the Stated, local government, business management and the like. Whether we look at commerce, the law, medicine, government or the 'people-work' or management professions like healthcare, teaching, welfare and social services, does not seem to make much difference. Professionals have often, it seems, come to be the 'hand-maidens' of the development of industrial capitalist society and socialist industrial societies alike.

It is perhaps not surprising, therefore, that sociologists have come to ask questions about the role of professions as exclusive, virtually self-perpetuating elites in society, while taking on and developing, perhaps, the characteristics of bureaucratic organisations central to the everyday management of society. Professionals have also, most importantly, been essential to the planning and policy-making processes within these dominating institutions of society. They have, as the facilitators of progress and technocrats of advanced industrial society, been in a position to shape the development of society very much in their own way. Although professionals are a small proportion of the total labour force in any industrial society they exert influence and control over their lives, rights and activities of many other workers. The autonomy and control of the professions may have been challenged in the last decade, but their indelible mark remains on our social structure.

Professionals have also often come to be, and to be seen as, the definers of the nature of social relations and human behaviour. Professionals *profess*; and in so doing create knowledge of a valued kind (Hughes, 63).

> "Routine definitions of ill-health, social
> adequacy, school achievement, degrees of
> criminality, for example, can be seen as
> grounded in the specific forms of expertness
> which at any one time are dominant

categories of thought which permeate over commonsense attitudes - as well as the power to enforce them - and are to some extent traceable to the political organisation of particular occupations, *e.g.* the judiciary, psychiatry and social work. Perhaps more important is the fact that professional legitimacy is often so strongly embedded and taken for granted that the cognitive frameworks within which we think about various social issues appear entirely self-evident and rational. Indeed, by appealing to a kind of universality and value neutrality in their knowledge, the professions put it in a sense beyond the social structures in which it has been formulated. In this way they portray a highly political process as non-political."

- Esland, *1977*

PROFESSIONS AND IDEOLOGY

The growth and increasing power of secular knowledge is a major factor in the modernisation processes. I mention this here because a good deal of what I want to argue in relation to the possible, likely or actual changes in the professions focuses attention upon the contradictions of the professions place in modern society. In *Facing up to Modernity*, Peter Berger comments on this issue.

> "In the contemporary world (this) dynamic
> of modernisation/counter modernisation is
> readily visible. There continues to be agg-
> ressive ideologies of modernity, confidently
> asserting that the *transformations* of our age
> are the birth pangs of a better life for
> humanity."
>
> - Berger, 1979

Professional ideologies are most certainly contemporary examples of this assertive modernity. Some of the central features of this dynamic that Berger refers to in 'Facing up to Modernity' are 'individuation'.

> "Modernisation has entailed a progressive
> separation of the individual from collective
> entities and as a result has brought about a
> historically unprecedented counter position
> of individual and society. This individuation
> is, as it were, the other side of the coin of…
> abstraction."
>
> - Berger *op. cit.*

For Berger this individuation runs contrary to the best interest of social welfare or well being. One of the issues raised by this section of my essay is the emphasis placed upon individual freedoms, operational autonomies and discretionary powers experienced and enjoyed by most professionals, which need to be addressed in any critical account of the professions and the likelihood of change. The acculturation process for most professionals actually inculcates and celebrates the (relative) autonomy of the professional.

In this sense, professions and professionals are seen as a major source of ideology production; creating the dominant ideas of and about society, and of and about themselves as essential to society.

Professionals have often been discussed in terms of their 'gate-keeper' role in the distribution of industrial societies' scarce resources. They have, after all, seemed in their role as experts to be the most appropriate people to make rational decisions about the distribution of scarce resources, human or material. The bureaucratic institutions that professionals have helped to create in the last hundred years have confirmed and reconfirmed the necessary roles of such experts of corporate management. I do not doubt that social scientists, including sociologists, have often been an integral part of this process. The writing of Mills (1959), O'Neill (1972), Gouldner (1971) or Bauman (1976), would all support the idea that sociology must be accountable and reflexive and that essentially sociology is a symbiotic science-profession whose promise is to give back to society an enhanced version of what it takes from them.

There are, however, contradictions inherent in any such social development and it is so here.

In this respect, the role of the professional is essentially political. Politics is about resources. It is about the allocation of resources and the decisions about allocation. It is about how power comes to be more the province of some indivi-duals and social groups than of others and how this fact affects resources. As social theorists, we are concerned with the social basis of politics, with, for example, how it is that some individuals or groups come to have more decision-making power than others. What is the history of these unequal relations, what forces are at work that seek or serve to maintain or change these situations? However, we can no longer just talk in conventional and traditional terms of the individual or of social class. We live in a time of bureaucratic organisations, some of which administer 'welfare'. Even when the government is dramatically changing the role of State Institutions the influence of these bureaucracies can be felt. Part of this change is an increasing split between bureaucratic and professional motivations, values, means and ends. What follows is an attempt to examine the nature and consequences of this split.

We have, within our welfare institutions, professional values, roles and personnel that have been brought about by modernising and often humanitarian forces-factors. These institutions are some of the 'sites of struggles', 'battle-grounds', for certain kinds of social change set against attempts to resist many such changes. We are also centrally concerned with the power these institutions have to make and shape ideas about decisions, about resources and their allocation. We are concerned with understanding the relationship between bureaucratic and professional ideas, practice and authority in these institutions.

One aspect of our interest and concern in this bureaucratic-professional split is that it was not always so self-consciously evident to the professionals themselves. In the first flush of development the institutional roles of social welfare provision, in the widest sense, were seen as good and positive - a clear moral posture embracing a set of ideas that reckoned the outcomes of these welfare interventions to be worth the administrative complexities. Less emphasis was placed on the organisational means than on the ends. The bureaucratic and professional were virtually collapsed together. In the last twenty years or so, the administrative process has become much more a significant issue: means have come to be the focus just as much as ends. Now this may be because professionals love to profess. As people have taken on professional roles they have 'fleshed them out' and made them much more 'a thing in themselves'.

However, it is important in these debates to acknowledge the arguments of those social theorists who see a distinctive difference between the traditional professions and the newer 'people-workers'. Bennett & Hockenstad, for example, argue that in two key respects, knowledge base and autonomy, the 'people-workers' are different. First, the knowledge base is more derived from and interrelated with, practice and the necessary skills developed by practitioners. These practice knowledges are seen by practitioner and client alike as a different kind of authority, an authority derived from the very service, which is given in a more democratic relation. Second, most 'people-workers' have been heirs to the social institutions developed by statutory and voluntary organisations since 1945. They are professional and yes, almost by definition, they are not self-employed, autonomous workers, they are employed by agencies of health and social services, education, *etc.*

Not surprisingly, therefore, this line of argument goes

some way towards an explanation of contradictions and conflicts that arise as a consequence of different interpretations of roles, means and ends between 'people-workers' and those that employ, administer or manage them (Bennett, W. S. and Hockenstad, M. C. in Halmos, 1973).

PROFESSIONS AND VESTED INTERESTS

We come back to a fundamental question. On whose behalf do the professions operate? Are they, in the pluralist's terms, merely carrying out a series of functions on behalf of society as a whole, the occupiers of these professional roles having been suitably 'qualified' to do so? Or are they, in the elitist theorist's terms, an inevitability of human social organisation, *i.e.* given any conglomeration of human beings, a few very significant organisers will always emerge as the appropriate facilitators of order? Or again, in the Marxist's terms, are they the well-paid lackeys of the ruling class (or ruling elite in the USSR, say) who have the degree of autonomy allowed them by the real economic and political rulers of society?

In terms of work and working, the role of professionals in manufacturing and service industries has become increasingly significant.

Sociologists of industry have turned their attention, for example, to the role of personnel managers - or, as Tony Watson (1977) has called them, 'the people-processors'. Watson, like Halmos (1970), has emphasised the important nature of this professional group's role as the providers of labour of suitable calibre. In the right place at the right time. These professionals are required to provide as rationally and cost-effectively as demanded, the appropriate units of labour power and yet, at one and the same time, need to keep themselves aware of the desires, needs and wants of workers of all kinds, including fellow professionals.

This group of aspiring professionals also reflect an important concern for sociologists of professions, namely the development and influence of the professional association. Whether we be talking of the British Medical Association or the Institute of Personnel Management or the RCN, it is possible to observe the 'gatekeeping' and regulatory function of such professional associations. These associations have invariably been dubbed the 'trade unions' of the professions, and there are some points of similarity in that the origins of both types of organisation can be seen to be derived from the medieval guild system, with its setting of standards for access, role as training agent, arbiter of general rules of conduct and facilitator of improved status, pay and conditions for its membership.

There is constantly a contradiction present between the professional as an individual; well educated, powerful and perhaps with a sophisticated lifestyle; and the professional as a member of an organisation, perhaps a bureaucracy. Sociologists have disagreed as to the extent that the authority claimed by and given to professions and professionals is based on rational criteria. Are they the most suitable people to make judgements about important features of others' lives? The professions themselves have invariably emphasised their necessarily exclusive and expert role, but many professionals may, in practice, find it difficult to make choices between the ethos and rules of conduct of their chosen profession, and the demand of the organisation that they work for. Many professionals do, for example, deliberately make public, issues, which the organisation they work for has considered best kept secret. This cannot only cause conflict for the professionals themselves, but can cause conflicts in the organisational or societal sphere as well. Peter Worsley has suggested that the role of 'professional' will tend to differ in societies where an underlying individualistic philosophy of possessive property ownership is 'replaced' by a collective response to social needs. This can be noted in societies like China or Mexico or Tanzania, where mass medical services are provided by large numbers of rudimentarily trained medical staff to supplement the existing core of highly qualified, temporarily scarce, professionals (Worsley, 1977).

We must not assume that because some sociologists have identified and discussed what they consider to be the dominance of professions and professionals, and that the professionals themselves often value highly their contribution, that the majority of people recognise this or accept it.

Johnson (1972) has emphasised this aspect of the debate on professionals in discussing 'trait' theory. This is the way in which many sociologists have drawn up a list of prominent functions of professions and professionals which is seen to outline their role and thereby their importance to progress and stability in society.

As Johnson points out, this has tended take the existence of professionals as an aspect of the division of labour and differentiation in society, for granted. It is a view that has tended to reinforce and even legitimates the professionals as an elite within an increasingly plural social order, without, in fact, raising the question of the nature of, and distribution of, economic and political power in society.

I would, however, want to add a note of caution in the ongoing debate about the professions, professionals and power. The last twenty years has seen considerable arguments presented by the likes of Illich, Braverman and Foucault on the power of the professions located in their knowledge base. Foucault and the other 'deprofessionalisers' have offered an influential panoptic view of professions arguing a tyrannical homogenous disciplinary apparatus. The work of Freidson, for example, has offered a consistently sceptical view. While acknowledging the profound changes that have taken place in industrial societies in relation to the professions, Friedson, like Bucher and Strauss, places much more emphasis on the structural sources of diversity, dissent and occupational segmentation. Freid-son argues that it is real individual human beings that are the reservoirs, the embodiment of knowledge and that these people are sustained by organised institutions. Freidson therefore places much less significance on 'self-employment' among the professions (Illich 77, Braverman 74, Foucault 74, Freidson 71 and 88, Bucher and Strauss 61).

It may be one project to 'de-professionalise' society; can we envisage a society without professionals in their present form? It is perhaps another project to seek to 'de-ideologise' the professions? Whether this is desirable or practical is one set of questions. Whatever view was expressed here, some notice would have to be taken of how it would be done.

Would professional education, pre- or in-service be the best hope? However, with the apparently unlimited enthusiasm of occupational groups and individuals to achieve professional status, is it likely that any counter policy to remove the symbolic and practical boundaries of these occupational cultures would stand much chance of success?

It is somewhat ironic if we have to wait for groups or individuals to become status conscious professionals before they look to argue against the weaknesses of their isolated position, or the very existence of professions in society. One other glaring example of inconsistency can be added. Many professions offer examples of the ideological imbalance of other professions. Many professions and professionals offer formal and informal critiques of other professions and professionals. They rarely turn that critique or analysis on themselves. Indeed, part and parcel of the endless social reproduction of social relations in our societies and the re-legitimation that certain groups get, is precisely because they so assiduously seek it!

I have already referred, in this section of my essay, to the 'problems' or contradictions associated with individuation or the distinctive ideas about autonomy that most professionals have. Before progressing it is necessary to identify some of the concerns that sociologists and other social theorists have expressed about this facet of modern life and attempts to understand it.

It is not at all unusual to see sociologists stating their belief in the 'self-society tension' concept derived essentially from the work of C. Wright Mills (1959). This analytical tool, having the sociological imagination to see it, have insight into it, and with it, has often been slightly reformulated as the concept of the dialectical relationship between society and individuals.

But what are these interrelations? Of what separable components/factors/variables are they composed? If there is a balance or balances to be struck between them, where does it lie? Which, for example, are the most significant factors to consider? Not the least important reason for wanting to know this would be in policy and social-personal change and development terms. Will the most significant factors for one person or group be the same for everyone? From what research has been done on ascribed and achieved status, life chances, *etc.*, it would seem very unlikely that everyone is the same for analytical purposes. Can we measure, account for and explain these various and varying factors using the same techniques of sociological analysis? Do we expect the outcomes to be the same if we argue that the inputs, even given patterns of similarity, are very different?

Culture(s) provide us with a further set of difficulties. Culture is traditionally used by sociologists to recognise how human beings, individually and collectively, resolve self-society contradictions. We are here moving into analytical terrain where meaning seems to become a much more significant aspect of our speculations. Not the least of concerns here is the extent to which human beings, individually and/or collectively take action in their reflection upon their situation (praxis). What is also significant here is the importance placed upon the concept of role in situating both ideas and material existence in the life course and chances of human beings.

The debate about meaning and ideas is crucial in any analysis of society and self. Certainly a good deal has been said over the years about which factors of any person's life is more determining, the material conditions of their everyday lives (and the relationships that are part and parcel of that) or the ideas that people have and the meanings that they generate. Clearly, an assumption is made that the more reflective a person or group is upon the material circumstances of everyday life, the more likely they are to generate critical meanings that will seek to challenge normative orders.

This assumption is associated with the degree of autonomy that the human mind has from the social structures of everyday life. So, yes, human beings create and reproduce, value and legitimate social structures, celebrate and revile sets of social relations, *etc.* Social structures offer a range of spheres of influence for thinking and doing. Cultures are replete with symbolic aspects of these lived, active experiences. These social structures should also be 'extended' to acknowledge the question of resources and the natural and physical environment that clearly affect people's lives.

One of the key issues, therefore, is what agents or agencies make a difference to society and self. At this juncture we might well ask how professionals are more or less likely to evaluate their roles and their place in the social structures that act as the dynamic context of professional practice. Contemporary British sociology has not been without its reflectors upon these concerns.

Basil Bernstein's Durkheim-inspired structuralist theorising about the transformation of cultures has been one such contribution that is relevant here. Bernstein's writing consistently focuses on the conditions of change or non-change and he is interested in the values that promote change or defend the status quo.

> "Bernstein argues that, in principle, contemporary state schools are in a process of change and transition - from social arrangements founded upon and manifest in, mechanical solidarity, to those associated with organic solidarity. Let us enumerate briefly those features of school organisation that Bernstein seeks to capture. Under the 'old' order, teacher and pupil roles are relatively fixed and determinate. Pupils, for example, are categorised, grouped and processed in terms of a few generic categories: age, sex and ability are major dimensions of such schemes. Units of social organisation are arranged in such a way as to maximise internal homogeneity, and the attributes used to classify pupils (and teachers) are regarded as fixed and stable. 'Ability', for example, will be treated as a more or less stable attribute, used to classify pupils in the same way across years and across school subjects. Pupils would thus be allocated to forms or streams on the basis of such measured ability: there would be little mobility between streams, and pupils in a

given stream or form would remain together for substantial amounts of their schoolwork. Under such conditions, pupils are placed within the school on the basis of what pass for ascribed roles or characteristics.

As schools shift in organisation and ideology towards principles of organic solidarity, on the other hand, the emphasis moves towards the establishment of achieved roles for pupils. 'Ability', for instance, will no longer be thought of as a fixed and generic attribute. Rather, ability will be portrayed as a process, which is realised in the context of learning, and of interaction between teachers and taught. Hence, ability may be thought to be manifested differently in various pedagogic contexts: pupils maybe placed in sets for different school subjects, for instance. They are less likely to be placed in fixed structural units, which uniquely define the individual pupil's position within the school. Pupil's roles are, therefore, more flexible - or at any rate potentially so. School careers are achieved in terms of individual biographies, rather than ascribed in terms of pre-determined structural attributes or classes (in the most general sense of that term).
A parallel shift is suggested for teachers' roles in school. Under conditions of

'mechanical' solidarity, the social arrangements of the staff tend to follow disciplinary or subject lines. Subject departments tend to define the teacher's role: here again we find it is a matter of ascription and professional attributes, which are socially defined as relatively fixed. But the order changeth. The teacher's role, Bernstein suggests, is increasingly fragmented: classroom teaching of school subjects is supplemented by wider pastoral and careers duties. As the range of school subjects taught also becomes increasingly diverse, so the division of labour within the teaching staff becomes more complex, diffused and fragmented. Here too then, the person's role or biography is one that is to be made actively or accomplished rather than being given.

These shifts are paralleled by changes in pedagogy, curriculum and social control. The teacher ceases to operate solely as the provider of standard routines and solutions, and becomes the creator of problems for the pupils to solve. Pedagogy thus stresses pupil-discovery and self-discovery. The means of learning are valued, as much as or more than, its ends."

- Atkinson, 1985

On the other side of the coin, Neil Keddie has considered an important social institution in the light of the individuation concerns.

In Adult Education: an ideology of individualism' (Keddie, 1980 in Thomson), Keddie argues that the claim for the 'uniqueness' of adult education as compared to the rest of education is an ideology that actually requires examination. Part of the current ideology of adult education is the student-centred, meeting the students-learners needs issue. Another linked issue for Keddie is the increasing emphasis on professionalisation.

> "The ideology of adult education achieves,
> for practitioners, a promise to their clientele
> that their primary concern will be with
> students' needs and interests; and equally
> important, it operates to combat the mar-
> ginality of adult education to the education
> system and helps to confirm practitioners'
> professional identities."
>
> - Keddie

Does the relatively low status of adult education threaten the professional identity or sense of self-worth of those practitioners engaged in it? What measures 'within' the conventional ideology might such professionals use to combat this? It would seem that, for the practitioners, most adult education is an attempt to reach those who have experienced the least formal education or had least opportunities. If this is true, then this is somewhat ironic in placing this activity in a context of social differentiation and access to education. In this sense, it is really a class issue! However, this class analysis runs contrary to the belief held in adult education about *continuing* education. But what is it that is being continued? Adult education is a *person*-centred, rather than a subject-centred activity. I raise this matter here because so much of the education of professionals also claims the same pedigree. Individual need rather than achievement becomes the focus. However, adult education, like professional education, reproduces the value(s) of individualism as expressed through access to education. Does this then create, reinforce and reproduce the contradictions of individualistic values compared with: (a) service *for* and within the community/society; and (b) the emancipation of a class through *social*, as distinct from individual, transformations?

As I have stated at the beginning of this section, the increased access to education and the professions has been seen as one of *the* fundamental examples of a more open and egalitarian society. But as we have seen, the critics of the professions are not convinced that has meant a better society or the liberation of our society from contradictions. Professionals continue to claim that they are altruistic and exist to give service to society rather than themselves. Most sociology is extremely sceptical of that claim and if we are on the threshold of a major reappraisal of the nature and role of the professional in our society, we must ask these questions. What is the bill of goods that society is to be sold in the era of the 'new professional'? One of my central concerns with the concept of the reflective practitioner is to ask precisely what qualitative differences in the nature, role and orientation of professional practitioners is anticipated as a consequence of a proposed rethinking of, and refocusing on, practice?

Bibliography

ALBERMARLE REPORT: *The Youth Service in England and Wales*, Ministry of Education, HMSO, 1960

ARGYRIS, C.: *Personality and Organisation - The Conflict between System and the Individual*, New York, Harper & Row, 1957

ARGYRIS, C. & SCHÖN, D. A.: *Theory in Practice: Increasing Professional Effectiveness*, Jossey-Bass Inc., San Francisco, 1974

ARGYRIS, C. & SCHÖN, D. A.: *Organisational Learning: A Theory of Action*, NY, Addison-Wesley, 1978

ARMSTRONG, D.: "The Way We Teach Medical Sociology" in Gomm, R. & McNeill, P., 1982

ASTLEY, John: *Culture & Creativity*, The Company of Writers, UK, 2006

ASTLEY, John: *Liberation & Domestication*: *Young People, Youth Policy and Cultural Creativity,* The Company of Writers, UK, 2006

ASTLEY, John: *Professionalism & Practice*, The Company of Writers, UK, 2006

ASTLEY, John: *Why Don't We Do it in the Road? The Beatles Phenomenon Explained*, The Company of Writers, UK, 2006

ASTLEY, J.: "The Sociology Teacher as Entertainer" in Lambe and Joseph, 1985

ASTLEY, J.: "Industrial-Urban Culture, Youth and the Problem of Socialisation" in *The Social Science Teacher*, Vol.8, No.2, 1978

ATKINSON, P.: "*Language, Structure and Reproduction: An Introduction to the Sociology of Basil Bernstein*, Methuen, London, 1982

AUSUBEL, D. P. (Ed's): *Educational Psychology: A Cognitive View*, Holt, Rinehart & Winston, New York, 1978

BALOGH, R. and BEATTIE, A.: *Performance Indicators in Nursing Education*, Final Report on a Feasibility Study, U.L.I.E., 1988

BARNES J.H. & LUCAS, H: *Positive Discrimination in Education: Individuals, Groups and Institutions*. In Barnes (Ed.) *Educational Priority* (Vol.3), HMSO, 1975

BARON, S. et. al.: *Unpopular Education. Schooling and Social Democracy in England (1944-1981)*, Hutchinson, 1981

BAUMAN, Z.: *Socialism: The Active Utopia*, Allen & Unwin, London, 1976

BEATTIE, A. "Making a Curriculum Work" in Allan and Jolley, 1987

BECKER, H. S., *et al* (Ed..): *Institution and the Person*, Aldine Publishing Co., Chicago, 1968

BENNETT, W. S. & HOKENSTAD, M. C.: "Full time People Workers and conceptions of 'the Professional'", in Halmos, 1973

BERGER, P. : *Facing up to Modernity*, Harmondsworth, Penguin, 1979

BERNSTEIN, BASIL: "Education Cannot Compensate for Society" in Cosin, Ben *et al* (Eds,), *School & Society*, Routledge & Kegan Paul, 1971

BLIGH, D. (Ed.): *Professionalism and Flexibility in Learning*, Guildford, S.R.H.E. Monograph, 1982

BOARD OF EDUCATION: Circular 1516, HMSO, 1940

BOARD OF EDUCATION: *The Youth Service after the War*, (first) Report of the Youth Advisory Council, HMSO', [see also MINISTRY OF EDUCATION for Second Report (J. Wolfenden was chairman for both Reports)], 1943

BRIGHOUSE, HARRY: *On Education*, Routledge, 2006

BRAVERMAN, H.: *Labour and Monopoly Capital*, New York, Monthly Review Press, 1974

BROOKFIELD, S. D.: *Developing Critical Thinkers*, Milton Keynes, Open University Press, 1987

BROWN, Muriel & MADGE, Nicola: *Despite the Welfare State*, Heinemann Educational Books, 1992

BRUNER, J. S.: *Research Program on Intellectual Development*, Harvard University Press, Cambridge Press, 1969

BUCKER, R. & STRAUSS, A.: "Professions in Process", *American Journal of Sociology* (66), Jan., 1961

BURT, C.: *The Young Delinquent*, ULP, 1969

CDP Inter-Project Editorial Team: *The Costs of Industrial Change* published by CDP, 1977

CLARKE, John & JOHNSON, Richard (Eds): *Working Class Culture*, Hutchinson, 1979

CLARK, J. & CRITCHER, C.: *The Devil Makes Work. Leisure in Capitalist Britain*, MacMillan, 1985

CLARKE, M.: "Action and Reflection: Practice and Theory in Nursing", *Journal of Advanced Nursing*, 11(1) p.3-11, 1986

COATES, Ken & SILBURN, Richard: *Poverty: The Forgotten Englishmen*, Penguin Special, 1970

COLLINI, Stefan: *Absent Minds: Intellectuals in Britain*, OUP, 2006

COLLINS, Michael: *The Likes of Us: A Biography of the White Working Class*, Granta Books, 2004

COOPER, C. L. (Ed.): *Theories of Group Processes*, Wiley, London, 1975

COULSON-THOMAS, C.: "Can Professions Adapt and Survive?" *Sunday Telegraph*, 5 March 1989.

CROSS, K. P.: *Accent on Learning: Improving Instruction, Reshaping the Curriculum*, Jossey-Bass, San Francisco, 1976

CROWTHER REPORT: (15 to 18), *p.36* , Min. of Ed. HMSO, 1959

DAVIS, B. D. (Ed.) *Research into Nurse Education*, London, Cross Helm, 1983

DAVIS, B. D. (Ed.): *Nursing Education: Research and Development*, London, Croom Helm, 1987

DAVID, F.: "Professional Socialisation as Subjective Experience: The Process of Doctrinal Conversion Among Student Nurses", in BECKER, 1968

DENCH, Geoff, GAVRON, Kate, YOUNG, Michael: *The New East End - Kinship, Race and Conflict*, Profile Books, 2006

DEWEY, J.: *How We Think: A Restatement of the Relation of Reflective Thinking to the Educative Process*, Henry Regnery, Chicago, 1933

DINGWALL, R. & LEWIS, P. (Ed's): *The Sociology of the Professions*, Macmillan , London, 1983

DOWIE, J. & ELSTEIN, D. (Ed's): *Professional Judgement*, Cambridge, CUP, 1988

EGGLESTON, J.: *Adolescence and Community: The Youth Service in Britain (p.16)*, Arnold, 1976

ESLAND, G. (Ed.): *People and Work*, Edinburgh, Holmes McDougall and Open University Press, 1977

FIELD, John: *Social Capital*, Routledge, 2003

FLETCHER, R.: *Family and Marriage in Britain*, Penguin, 1962.

FOUCALT, M.: *Archaeology of Knowledge*, Tavistock, London 1974

FRAYN, Michael: "Festival" in Sissons & French, 1963

FUREDI, Frank: "Confronting the New Misanthropy" Spiked *Essays* (online), 2006

FRIEDSON, E.: *Profession of Medicine: A Study of the Sociology of Applied Knowledge*, University of Chicago, 1970

FRIEDSON, E: *Professional Powers: A Study of the Institutionalisation of Formal Knowledge*, University of Chicago, 1988

FULLER, Roger & Stevenson, Olive: *Policies, Programmes and Disadvantage: A Review of the Literature*, Heinemann Educational Books, 1983

FYVEL, T.R. *The Insecure Offenders: Rebellious Youth in the Welfare State*, Penguin, 1961

FYVEL, T.R. : "The 'Insecure Offenders' in Retrospect" (p.128), *New Society*, 20 July 1978

GAGNE, R. M.: The *Conditions of Learning*, Holt, New York, 1977

GALLIE, D.: *Employment in Britain*, Oxford, Blackwell, 1989

GERTH, Hans & Mills, C. Wright: *Character and Social Structure*, Routledge & Kegan Paul, 1954

GITLIN, A. & TEITELBAUM, K.: *Linking Theory and Practice: The Use of Ethnographic Methodology by Prospective Teachers, Journal of Education for Teachin*g, 9(3), p.225-34, 1983

GLEN, S.: Do Nurse Teachers really want to Educate for care? From MA Thesis (unpublished), *Nursing Moral Education for the 3 C's: Care*, Concern and Correction, U.L.I.E., 1988

GOFFMAN, E.: *The Presentation of Self in Everyday Life*, Harmondsworth, Penguin, 1959

GOLDTHORPE, J.: *Class Structure in Modern Britain*, Oxford, Clarendon Press, 1987

GOMM, R. & MCNEILL, P. (Eds.): *Handbook for Sociology Teachers*, Heinemann, London, 1982

GOODE, W. J. *Exploration in Social Theory*, The Free Press, New York, 1973

GOODMAN, J.: *Reflection and Teacher Education: A Case Study and Theoretical Analysis*, Interchange, 15(3) p.9-25, 1984

GOULDNER, A.: *The Coming Crisis of Western Sociology*, London, Heinemann, 1971

GRANT, N.: "Citizen Soldiers: Army Education in World War 2" in *Formations of Nation and People*, Ed. by Bennett, T. *et al* RKP, 1984

GRANT, C. A. (Ed.): *Preparing for Reflective Teaching*, Allyn, London, 1984

HABERMAS, J.: *Knowledge and Human Interests*, London, Heinemann, 1978

HALMOS, P.: (Ed.): "Professionalisation and Social Change, Sociological Review Monograph, No.20, 1973.

HALMOS, P.: *The Personal and the Political - Social Work and Political Action*, Hutchinson, London, 1978

HABERMAS, Jurgen: *The Theory of Communicative Action* Cambridge, 1984

HALL, S.: *Reformism and the Legislation of Consent in Permissiveness and Control*: *the fate of the Sixties Legislation*. Edited by J. Clark, *et al*. MacMillan, 1980.

HALSEY, A.H., Heath A. & Ridge J.M: *Origins and Destinations*, Clarendon Press, 1980

HELLER, A.: *The Theory of Need in Marx*, Allison and Busby, London, 1976

HENDERSON, M. S. (Ed.): *Nursing Education* (Recent Advances in Nursing 4), Churchill-Livingstone, Edinburgh, 1982

HIRST, P. & WOOLLEY, P.: *Social Relations and Human Attributes*, Tavistock, London, 1982

HOLMES, J.: *Professionalisation - a misleading myth?*, N.Y.B., Leicester, 1981

HOUSE, E.: "Technology versus Craft' in Taylor, 1979

HUGHES, E.: "Professions" (1963) in Daedalus, Vol. 92, No.4, Autumn, 1973.

HUGHES, E., et al: Education for the Professions, New York, McGraw-Hill, 1973

HUMPHRIES, B.: "Adult Learning in Social Work Education: towards liberation or domestication", in Critical Social Policy, Issue 23, Vol. 8, No. 2, Autumn, 1988

ILLICH, Ivan: Deschooling Society, Harper & Row, 1971

ILLICH, Ivan.: Disabling Professions, M. Boyars, London, 1977

ILLICH, Ivan: Tools for Conviviality, Calder & Boyars, 1973 (1975 in Fontana)

JACKSON, Brian & MARSDEN, Dennis: Education and the Working Class Routledge, 1962 (Pelican 1966)

JACKSON, Brian: Streaming: An Education System in Miniature, Routledge & Kegan Paul, 1964

JACKSON, P. & MARSDEN, D.: Education and the Working Class, Harmondsworth, Penguin, 1962.

JARRELL, R.: A Sad Heart at the Supermarket, Farrar, Straus & Giroux, 1962.

JARVIS, P.: Professional Education, Croom Helm, London, 1983

JEFFS, A. J.: Young People and The Youth Service, RKP, 1979

JOHNSON, T.: Professions and Power, London, Macmillan, 1972

KEDDIE, N.: "Adult Education: an ideology of individualism" in Thompson, 1980

KILMINSTER, R.: Praxis and Method, RKP, London, 1979

KNOWLES, M.: The Adult Learner: A Forgotten Species, Croom Helm, London, 1973

KNOWLES, M.: "Androgogy: an emerging technology for Adult Learning" in Tight, 1983

KOLB, D. A. and FRY, R.: "Towards an Applied Theory of Experimental Learning" in Cooper, C. L. (Ed.), 1975

KOLB, D. A., ROBIN, I. M. & MCINTYRE, J. M.: Organisational Psychology - A Book of Readings, Prentice-Hall, Englewood Cliffs, 1979

KOLB, D. A.: *Experimental Learning. Experience as the Source of Learning and Development*, Englewood Cliffs, Prentice-Hall, 1984

KUNDERA, Milan: *The Art of the Novel*, Faber, 1988

LAMBE, K., & JOSEPH, M. (Ed's): Teaching Sociology to non-Sociologists. Oxford School of Business, 1985

LARKIN, R.W. *Suburban Youth in Cultural Crisis*, OUP, 1979

LEWIS, Jeremy: *The Life and Times of Allen Lane*, Penguin Press, 2005

LEFEBVRE, Henri: *The Sociology of Marx*, Allen Lane, The Penguin Press, 1968

LEONARD, P.: *Personality and Ideology*, London, Macmillan, 1984

LAW, M. & RUBENSON, K.: "Andragogy: the Return of the Jedi, in S.C.U.T.R.E.A", 1988

MacINTYRE, Alisdair: *Marcuse*, Fontana, 1970

MacINTYRE, A.: *After Virtue: A study in moral theory*, London, Duckworth, 1981

McEVOY, P.: "Prepare for Project 2000" in *Nursing Times* (p.40-1), Vol.85, No.6, 8 February, 1989

McILROW, J.: *A Critical Theory of Adult Learning and Education in Adult Education*, Vol.32, No.1, Washington, 1981

McROBBIE, Angela: *The Uses of Cultural Studies*, Sage, 2005

MAYS, J.: *The Young Pretenders*. Sphere, 1969

MARWICK, Arthur: *Culture in Britain since 1945*, Blackwell, 1991

MILLERSON, G.: *The Qualifying Associations: A Study of Professionalisation*, RKP, London, 1984

MINISTRY OF EDUCATION: *The Purpose and Content of the Youth Service*, Report (second) of the Y.A.C., HMSO, 1945

MOSLEY, Ivo   (Ed.): *Dumbing Down: Culture, Politics and the Mass Media*, Thorverton, 2000

MILLS, C. W.: The *Sociological Imagination*, Harmondsworth, Penguin, 1959

NARR, W. D.: *Pluralistiche Gesellschaft* (Pluralist Associations), Gessell, Hanover, 1969

NEAL, D.: "The First Year of a CQSW Course" in Gomm and McNeill, 1982

O'NEILL, J.: *Sociology as a Skin Trade*, London, Heinemann, 1972

PACKARD, Vance: The *Hidden Persuaders*, 1957

PACKARD, Vance: *The Waste Makers*, Pelican, 1960

PANNICK, D.: "Reforming the Legal Profession", *The Guardian*, 14 April 1989.

PLOWDEN REPORT: *Children and their Primary Schools: A Report of the Central Advisory Council for England* (Vol 1). 1967

POSTMAN, Neil: *Amusing Ourselves to Death*, Penguin Education, 1986

RUBINSTEIN, David & STONEMAN, Colin: *Education for Democracy*, Penguin Education, 1970

SCHAMA, Simon: *A History of Britain* Episode 3 (1776–2000): The Fate of Empire, BBC, 2003

SCUTREA: Papers from the Transatlantic Dialogue, Leeds Conference, July 1988.

SEABROOK, Jeremy: "The Great Consumer Swindle", *The Guardian*, 21 August 1982

SENNET, Richard: *The Corrosion of Character*, W.W. Norton, 1998

SHOTTER, J.: *Social Accountability and Selfhood*, Blackwell, Oxford, 1984.

SILLITOE, A.: *Saturday Night and Sunday Morning*, Pan, 1958

SIMPKIN, M.: *Trapped within Welfare*, London, Macmillan, 1979

SISSONS, Michael & FRENCH, Philip (Ed's.) *Age of Austerity* (1945-1951), Hodder, 1963 (Penguin 1964)

TAYLOR, P. H. (Ed.): *New Directions in Curriculum Studies*, Falmer Press, Brighton 1979

THOMPSON, J. L. (Ed.): *Adult Education for a Change*, Hutchinson, London, 1980

TIGHT, M. (Ed.): *Education for Adults* (Vol.1), Adult Learning in Education, Croom Helm, London, 1983.

WALKER, A. and WESTERGAARD, J.: "Cross Currents in Views of Welfare: Prospects for Socialist Change." Unpublished paper to Socialism and Social Policy Conference, Leeds Polytechnic, 1988

WATSON, T. J.: *The Personnel Managers: A Study in the Sociology of Work and Employment*, RKP, London, 1977.

WILLIAMS, Raymond: *Culture*, Fontana, Glasgow, 1981

WILLIAMS, Raymond: *The Country and the City*, Chatto & Windas, 1973 (Hogarth Press, 1985)

WILLIS, Paul: *Common Culture*, The Open University Press, 1990

WILLIS, Paul: *Learning to Labour*, Saxon House, 1978

WILLIS, Paul: *Moving Cultures*, Calouste Gulbenkian Foundation, 1990

WILLIAMSON, J. A. (Ed.): *Current Perspectives in Nursing Education. The Changing Scene*, The C. V. Mosby Company, Saint Louis, 1976

WORSLEY, P.: *Introducing Sociology*, Penguin, Harmondsworth, 1977.

YOUNG, Michael: *The Rise of the Meritocracy*, Penguin, 1961

YOUNG, M. F. D. (Ed.): *Knowledge and Control*, Collier Macmillan, London, 197)

ZEICHNER, K. M: "On Becoming a Reflective Teacher" in Grant, C. A. (Ed.): *Preparing for Reflective Teaching*, 1984

ZEICHNER, K. M.: *Journal of Education for Teaching*, Vol.12, No.1, p.5-24, 1986

ZEICHNER, K. M. & TEITELBAUM, K.: "Personalised and Inquiry Oriented Teacher Education: An Analysis of Two Approaches to the Development of Curriculum for Field Based Experiences", Journal of Education for Teaching", 8(2), p.95-117, 1982

ZWEIG, F.: *The British Worker*, Penguin, 1952.

Index

NOTES

NOTES